THE INTENTIONAL BUSINESS

Molly McKinley

Art by Tory Elena

Design by Beth Brant

To my family; Connor, Cate, Will, Rand, Mimi and Pops, for all the things. I love you with every cell of my being. To my long time teacher and friend, Dharma, for guiding me on the path. To Debra for your unending support and sisterhood. To Beth, who is always the first one to say, "Let's do it." Thank you.

"Everything great starts as somebody's daydream."

-UNKNOWN

TABLE OF CONTENTS

Foreword by Debra Trappen	5
A Letter to the Reader	9
Yamas & Niyamas	17
The Yamas	23
Ahimsa	
Satya	
Asteya	
Brahmacharya	
Aparigraha	
The Niyamas	53
Saucha	
Santosha	
Tapas	
Svadhyaya	
Ishvara Pranidhana	
The Power of Intention	77
Nature's Blueprint	101
The Heart of It All	131
Intentional Marketing	139
Putting It Into Action	181

FOREWORD BY DEBRA TRAPPEN

I am honored to have the opportunity to write this foreword for my beloved friend, Molly McKinley's brilliant book, *The Intentional Business*. I believe this book will become a guiding light for a new generation of soul-centered business owners, a beacon for those who are looking for a fresh, more collaborative, and socially conscious way of building a business. In a world where profit consistently comes before people or purpose, we need a recipe for change - and she weaves hers into these pages.

Molly and I met over a decade ago while both working in the real estate industry. She was filming interviews with agents and leaders who were making a difference in their markets - telling their stories to inspire others to build their business with authenticity and purpose. When I reflect on our beginning, her passion for connecting people and brands in a truly magical and intentional way has always been incredibly clear. This book reflects her heart for serving others and sharing her wisdom. She truly believes, with intentionality, we can harness the power of a focused mind and push beyond predetermined, patriarchal limitations placed upon us by ourselves and others.

Over the last few years, our connection and collaborations have expanded and deepened. We host a talk show together where the topic of intentional business is always on her lips. She truly lives and breathes this work. Molly has helped me numerous times to realign my soul-centered consulting business visions and uncover ways to take my ideas to the next level through partnerships and philanthropy. Whenever I ask questions (and I ask a lot of them) she consistently provides thoughtful advice and then circles back around to how that advice would help her other clients and community. It was a blessing to be walking alongside her as she wrote and edited the final pages and iterations of this book and can attest to how much of her heart and soul are on each page.

Whether you are just starting your own business or on your 22nd startup, there is something in here for you. In The Intentional Business, Molly shares stories of her personal and professional journey building, growing, and closing businesses. She will give you the tools to reimagine your vision, connect the dots between your purpose and your marketing, infuse archetypes, and create positive ripples that continue for years to come.

You don't need to be a marketing genius or a pedigreed executive to accomplish the remarkable task of building an intentional business. Molly's advice weaves together Nature's principles, a spiritual knowing, and simple, practical advice that helps business owners, like you and me, become more intentional with each and every decision. Ultimately, you will learn how to see your business through the eyes of a Yogi, a gardener, and a fully divine-fully human being.

If you are exhausted by the senseless hustle or the hamster wheel you just can't seem to get off and are ready to create your own table with your own rules - the insight in this book will help you heal and design the plan to get you there. The journal prompts, meditations, and calls to concentrate you hold in your hands will keep you focused and help you soak in all of her wisdom and wit.

If you're ready to honor your soul's purpose in and through your business - now is the time, this book is your guide.

Debra Trappen is an intuitive guide, best-selling author, retreat creator, and a respected voice of women's empowerment movements. She is a lover of wild women, soul sessions, haikus, books, magic, moxie, tea, and wine.

"I am not interested in picking up crumbs of compassion thrown from the table of someone who considers himself my master. I want the full menu of rights."

—DESMOND TUTU

A LETTER TO THE READER

Dear Reader,

Simply put, I don't want a seat at this table anymore. I want to build a new one altogether.

This is written for anyone who has sat around a board table, a leadership table, a conference table and wondered why we have to play by this set of rules we inherited. For anyone who looked at the faces they were building with and wondered how in the heck they got there. For anyone brave enough to listen to their bones crying out for a different way, a new path, and a way of doing business that values more than growth for the sake of growth alone.

This book is for you, the female entrepreneur, who has been unheard, marginalized and unfunded. Yet, you still persist with a vision for a business that can create right living for yourselves and your family. Where your business itself is aligned with your values, where your time and energy is well-spent and also gives back to the community it serves. This is for the co-creators, who know that we are only limited by our imaginations and who hear the call for change. For the door-kickers who will never accept that this is just how things are supposed to be. For the creatives, who are willing to look at constraints as opportunities to problem solve with deep, thoughtful, soulful solutions.

This is for the woke men who realize that women are worthy of investment dollars and know that our world is out of balance. Who understand that supporting women in business will create a rich, diverse, and much needed texture to our society. For the men who also sit at the tables they have inherited and wonder how in the heck they got there. For the men who feel the pressure to check their gut at the door for the sake of kowtowing to investors and board members.

Let's start this conversation off with some hard truth-telling. The way I see it, most business leaders lose their way for one primary reason, greed. Whether it's their own greed or the greed of others pulling the strings. Greed is a tough word to swallow because after all, businesses are supposed to make money. Its Old English origination nods to "voracious hunger," and is applicable in its essence of never being enough. Somewhere along the journey, the original vision and intention for why the business was created is diluted for more, more and more. It can happen in all sorts of ways, but the soul of the business is slowly suffocated. A personal example of how easily this can happen is with the launch of my own brand, Intentionaliteas. I had a vision for this business, it came to me, along with a clear plan for the business and the life I wanted to build. The tea blends would be based on intention and the herbs would support the intention. I would sustainably farm the herbs and create goodness loops, a built-in way to give back to a cause aligned with the intention of each different tea blend. But the pressure and realities of having to bring in money to pay bills and to provide for my family quickly shifted the vision. The first thing I cut was the goodness loop, and started to adjust the product to what I thought I could sell, instead of what I wanted to create. Since then, I have pivoted and tacked, shifted and adjusted, all while searching for marketshare and profitability. I finally concluded that for the meantime, my primary source of income needed to come from another source so I could remain true to the vision I set off on when I began the tea journey. I had to let things steep, so to speak.

Available resources often guide our decision-making and can lead us down a slippery path we do not want to be on. When we are able to remain neutral and rise above the turbulence into clear thinking, we can see opportunities that may be lost to others stuck in the storm. It requires steadfast focus and vision to create a business, let alone an intentional business, which we will explore together throughout the following pages. Often, the business of our dreams may look different than the path we originally set on. Do not misunderstand, your business can and should be profitable, but we will take a look and redefine what it means to be "profitable." The root word of profit is from Latin profectus, meaning to advance or to progress. Our businesses have the unique opportunity to advance society, the way we care for each other, our communities, and contribute to the whole in a profound way. To progress society, our spirit, and the world. I'm hoping this book will provide a new and fulfilling framework so we can keep our attention on the aspects that are life-giving, as opposed to that which depletes.

The process of learning to listen to the whisper of the quiet internal voice, instead of the louder, clumsier voice that usually commands our full attention, is a profound investment in yourself. I clearly remember the moment when I was asked to present a marketing strategy for the board of investors at a startup that I had signed on to assist. The room was hot and stuffy, the laminate table was bleak and crowded, the men were jockeying for alpha position, and as the only woman in the room, I felt woefully out of place. Not because I wasn't worthy of playing with these people, but because I didn't want to. I was over it. This was not the face of business that fired me up. These were not the conversations that ignited my soul. These were not the people that I admired. I was done. It was finally time for me to launch a business that truly reflected my soul and to walk the path of purpose and prosperity.

My intention for this book is to help others walk a path toward creating businesses aligned with their soul's highest purpose. My hope is that we can reimagine how we spend our best hours of the day and how we earn a living so it's not decoupled from our spiritual Selves. For too long, we have lived in the duality of our personal and professional lives, trying to keep these parts separate. But it's time to integrate these two aspects of our being into one whole picture of the work we were not only born to do, but the work that is deeply fulfilling and can bring change and healing to ourselves, to others, and to our living planet. John Mackey, co-founder and CEO of Whole Foods Market, co-founded the Conscious Capitalism Movement and co-authored a

New York Times and Wall Street Journal best-selling book entitled Conscious Capitalism, Liberating the Heroic Spirit of Business. His book is a wonderful example of a successful entrepreneur who understands the potential impact when we re-imagine capitalism, not only for the community and customers but employees as well.

The next generation of successful businesses in the age of Aquarius will understand that doing good is good business. Enlightened entrepreneurs who know who they are and are directing their will with their intention are the new creators. We have the choice to wield our energies with purpose and clarity or we can continue on a path of reaction and disconnection.

As you walk through these pages, you are welcome to skip around, jump ahead, and follow your intuition about what to read. This book is nonlinear, meaning you don't have to read it in any particular order. Each segment is a new idea with its own journal prompts, meditations and intentions. These questions are a culmination of questions I have asked myself about my own businesses over the years, as well as the questions I wish I would have asked earlier. You can use the journal to go as deep as you need to go because the commitment to self reflection is profoundly helpful. You have your own answers, these questions will assist in this excavation. It's my hope you will come back to the different segments whenever there is uncertainty, so you can refocus and realign with your internal vision.

If you do not have a current meditation practice, and these instructions feel foreign or uncomfortable, I encourage you to visit our website, intentionaltogether.com for audio and video guided instructions. Starting a meditation practice can be uncomfortable physically, mentally and emotionally but is worth every ounce of effort to turn your attention within and learn to listen to the still-small voice inside. Creating a special space in your home or office to do this work will help greatly. Try to reduce any distractions, outside noise and material clutter. Turn off any technology that may pull you away from focus. Establishing a ritual, the root of spi*ritual*ity, is a wonderful way to prepare your mind, through repetitive actions, to focus your energy and effort.

My personal ritual is to brew a cup of tea, light a candle, and sit quietly at an altar I've constructed away from the hustle of my family life. An altar can be as simple or as complex as you desire, just follow your intuition to create a space that is comfortable, safe, free from distraction, and speaks to you. A simple table with fresh flowers or a plant is a beautiful place to start. The easier it is to focus your mind, the easier it will be to direct your energy with intention. Learning to direct your energy with intention is the key to creating a business of your dreams, aligned with your highest purpose, and to becoming abundantly prosperous.

So let's be intentional together.
Molly

"Morality, like art, means drawing a line someplace."

–OSCAR WILDE

THE YAMAS & NIYAMAS

While on my personal yogic journey, I found myself constantly thinking how applicable yogic philosophy would be for business. I caught myself applying the spiritual principles to my work and drawing parallels to the implications if we could operate this in business and daydreaming about how much more fulfilling our work lives could be. We have a tendency to compartmentalize our personal selves and our business selves, when the reality is that we are one person expressing different aspects of who we are based on the experience at hand. So, how in the world does yoga apply to business? Let me explain.

When I was in the midst of my yoga teacher training, we took a deep dive into the *Yoga Sutras of Patanjali*. This book, written by the father of yoga, outlines the core values of the practice in eight essential paths, otherwise known as limbs. These limbs include yama (abstinences), niyama (observances), asana (yoga postures), pranayama (breath control), pratyahara (withdrawal of the senses), dharana (concentration), dhyana (meditation) and samadhi (absorption).

In our Western understanding of yoga, we think of poses and postures to strengthen and tone the body, but the original Eastern intent was much more profound. The aim of yoga was to unite the breath, body, and spirit to achieve the highest possible state of existence: samadhi, nirvana or enlightenment. For many entrepreneurs this is what we want for our businesses.To spend our waking, working hours on something that reflects our whole

Selves and create meaningful businesses aligned with purpose. Many would agree spending time on anything else seems like an incredible waste of energy and personal resources.

Before one could even begin a physical yoga practice, the aspiring student has to master the foundation of yama and niyama, the first two of the eight-limbed practices outlined by Patanjali. For the past twelve years, I've studied each of these abstinences and observances and believe them to be a solid foundation for creating a shared language for morals and ethics in business regardless, of spiritual tradition. These ideas represent basic ways of right living with yourself and right living with others.

I do not claim to be a moral authority. In fact, the older I become, the more I realize how unique and beautiful the lenses from which we individually perceive the world truly are. And, I have no desire to try to convince you that my lens is somehow better than yours. However, when building a business, it's critical to have a shared vision with our collaborators. Therefore, we have to create a shared language, something we can each individually understand so we can come together to create that collective drum beat of alignment.

Part of the process of delving deep into these yamas and niyamas and the application to business was interviewing numerous CEOs, business leaders and spiritual teachers that I have come to know and respect over the years. I was looking to discover if these individuals subscribed to one of these ideas as their ethos, their beacon or north star. What I discovered is that the current common framework is, "Do unto others as you would want done to you." The understanding and the application of The Golden Rule was the common thread of the people I interviewed and respect. This is a great start for the foundation of an intentional business. Do unto others is a reminder that the heart of businesses aren't products or services, but the people who invent, design and solve for the business. We lose our way when we forget the humans who create.

And, when we're dealing with humans, we have to remember that we all come from such diverse and different backgrounds. We were parented or not parented in numerous ways, so our boundaries and guideposts are all over the place. We have to constantly remind ourselves that every single moment in this particular life and body experience has shaped the way we perceive our surroundings. Our prior experiences, our drive, our hunger, all taint the way we see the world and our willingness to achieve or succeed. Many people still unconsciously subscribe to the notion of success "by any means necessary" out of sheer competition and fear of failure. I too, am a competitive person that wants to win, but am redefining and creating a new perspective on what winning and failure actually look like.

So, when we establish clear communication about our common language and set clear expectations of what the means of success, building and collaboration look like, we ensure that we create an understood and agreed-upon light post to reduce the uncertainty of the vagaries and grayness of morals and ethics. As we dive into these ancient ideals, let's remember that as long as we are in human bodies, there is shared understanding that we are a work in progress. Mastery of all of these is an aspiration. Grace with ourselves and each other as students and aspirants is equally important. A friend and respected business leader summed it up perfectly when he received negative pushback when he published his book. Armchair critics were quick to jump on apparent idiosyncrasies of his ideals, the intended action and the actual outcomes. He said he wished he had stated his thoughts with a question mark instead of a period. That way, the spirit of his words could land the way he hoped instead of being perceived as finger pointing and finger wagging.

Therefore, as we discuss and discover the yamas and niyamas as a potential common framework to create a solid foundation for business regardless of spiritual, ethical or moral backgrounds, we are coming together as students with curiosity and question marks. My fingers are tucked in my pockets in case you need a visual.

"As you start to walk on the way, the way appears"

—RUMI

THE YAMAS

The yamas are primarily concerned with our world and our interactions with each other, basically, how we treat each other. It's an important place to start because if we follow these guidelines, we most certainly will bring a layer of intention and care into our businesses. The yamas allow us to pay attention and value the interconnectedness of the business with the people and community that it serves. When we do this, we bring our humanity to the forefront.

"The roots of all goodness lie in the soil of appreciation for goodness."

—DALAI LAMA

AHIMSA

The first yama is Ahimsa, or non-harming. All other yamas and niyamas bow to the idea of doing no harm. At times, when faced with complex issues, it's easy to get lost in the decision-making tree. Using Yamas and Niyamas as our roadmap, the simple answer to the question, "Does this cause harm to ourselves, to our customers, to our community, to our planet, to anything?" can help guide us on our path. This is an important and often overlooked question for business, but is the single most important aspect of becoming an intentional business. When we take a hard look at our business lives in the world, we can determine if there are ways we can solve for collateral damage resulting from the business itself.

Another way of looking at ahimsa is not just about causing or not causing harm, but rather, bringing life to something. With this layer of intent, we can ask, "How does our business bring life to our employees, our customers, our community, and our planet?" This lens of honesty and transparency will shed light on the true value the business serves. This type of soul-searching will provide the hooks needed to weave a compelling and collective narrative throughout all messaging and marketing.

But let's face it, we cause harm all the time, knowingly and unknowingly. It's nearly impossible not to. If you have a business that creates products, it's more likely than not that we are harming the planet in some way. If you send mailers, postcards, or print brochures for marketing, you're killing trees.

If you travel to speak or attend trade shows, you harm the environment through carbon emissions. We harm ourselves with negative self-talk and often this frustration spills onto others in outbursts. Unfamiliarity creates fear, fear creates imbalances and imbalance creates harm. When we start to really look at ahimsa, it can put us in an immediate state of defeat or apathy because it's such a big idea with tons of trickle up and down implications. That being said, awareness is key. I believe that by even asking the question and acknowledging the fact that our businesses will inherently create both good and harm, we can begin candid and honest dialogue about how to improve and solve for the known areas where our business takes more than it gives.

As a long-time vegetarian, who practices ahimsa as it relates to food choice and non-harming of animals for my consumption, it reminds me of a common snarky question I get when I explain why I don't eat meat. "Well, don't you care about the plants you kill, don't you harm those when you eat them?" Yes, the plants do die to nourish us and that should be acknowledged. However, the wisdom comes when we think about choosing foods that are grown and harvested in a sustainable way. Purchasing products that don't have unnecessary packaging and plastics that will be tossed and cause future harm, to compost what we haven't eaten, so that eventually we give back to the earth what we've taken from it.

I've struggled a ton with ahimsa because harm and pain seem to be so prevalent in our culture, but I have landed with the understanding that awareness is the first step to creating life-giving solutions. Life-giving solutions create balance and balance is the root of compassion, empathy and unconditional love. Yes, these ideas are as important to the soul of intentional businesses as they are to our individual Selves. After all, remember a business is a collective group of people solving problems and creating services for other people. So why should these ideals be excluded?

JOURNAL PROMPTS

1. What are the areas of my business that we could potentially do harm?
2. Do these areas do more harm than good?
3. Are we bringing life to this situation or creating pain?
4. Who does this harm and how can we make amends?
5. Do I harm myself in any way—physically, emotionally, spiritually, financially—by working in this manner?

MEDITATION

Come to a quiet, seated pose. Exhale down your spine and imagine a root digging deeply into the earth. Anchor this root and imagine sister roots stretching far and wide under the dirt. Inhale deeply and find extra length in your spine, reaching tall through the crown. Imagine tree branches with colorful leaves and fruit growing from your head. Bring your awareness to the color of the leaves, what do you see? Bring your awareness to the fruit on the branches. What do you see? Return to your breath and feel the air entering and leaving your nose. Slowly blink your eyes open. Journal whatever images came to your awareness.

INTENTIONAL AFFIRMATION

My business is life giving.

"A lie would make no sense unless the truth was felt to be dangerous."

—CARL JUNG

SATYA

Satya is truthfulness and may be the grayest of gray zones in our current business culture. As a marketer, I am more than guilty of creating aspirational language when the product may not quite live up to the narrative I've created. We pass this off as storytelling, as creative messaging, or as spinning. Many of us have at some point subscribed to the "fake it till you make it" ideology while we are inventing or reinventing our businesses.

So what's the big deal? What are we so afraid of that we are willing to risk our reputation for half-truths and even blatant lies?

It's my opinion that the fear of failure is the root of our dishonesty. There is such incredible pressure to perform, to showcase an up-and-to-the-right data story, that we are willing to tweak numbers, withhold information and shape a different narrative for the sake of appearing successful. Every single business originated from some person or person's daydream at some point in time. Despite the size or the stage of the company, creating an illusion of success, demand and interest is critical to actually creating success, demand and interest. Or is it?

When businesses cook the books, misappropriate resources, or aren't transparent in their business practices, everyone loses. Unless we change the mentality of success at all costs to a more holistic expectation of the natural ebbs and flows of a business, where there is safety in creating clear, articulate, accurate representations of what actually is.

That being said, truth is tricky because we all see the world so radically differently. As humans, we often do not see the entirety of truth, just the aspect of truth that we have seen or understand. To be seekers of truth requires us to clean our lenses from time to time. Only when we swap glasses with those beside and alongside us can we see things from new perspectives. Through this process, we will hopefully have the courage to look clearly, without judgment, always challenging and questioning our own assumptions. This is how we can grow together, when we are unafraid of the unnamed threat that lurks behind the willingness to see and call things for what they are.

Truth asks that we remove our masks. That we show up with radical self-acceptance for the bright parts of our being but also the shadowy, more protected parts of ourselves that we hide in fear of judgment. We cannot build together unless we embrace radical honesty about what we do well and where others should take the reins so that they can step into their zone of genius. We'll uncover this more later.

JOURNAL PROMPTS

1. What areas of my business are being spun, pumped up or glazed over?
2. Where do I give myself permission to hide business details?
3. What am I afraid of, by revealing things as they are?
4. How does my culture support truthfulness?
5. Are my employees able to be free in who they are? How do they hide their wholeness?

MEDITATION

Come to a quiet, seated pose. Exhale down your spine and imagine a root digging deeply into the earth. Anchor this root and imagine sister roots stretching far and wide under the dirt. Inhale deeply and find extra length in your spine, reaching tall through the crown. Begin to visualize yourself seated in meditation, like you are looking at a reflection of yourself. What do you see? What masks are you wearing? What imagery is in the shadows?

Return to your breath and feel the air entering and leaving your nose. Slowly blink your eyes open. Journal whatever images came to your awareness.

INTENTIONAL AFFIRMATION

My business reflects the highest truth.

"Reflect upon your present blessings, of which every man has plenty; not on your past misfortunes, of which all men have some."

—CHARLES DICKENS

ASTEYA

The next yama is Asteya, or non-stealing, which is essential to the idea of building businesses in the spirit of truth and reciprocity. We steal from ourselves and our future by being over-leveraged with debt. We steal ideas and recognition from others. We steal from our planet by not replacing the resources we use. We steal from each other in a million subtle and not so subtle ways.

As black and white as something like truth and lies may seem on the surface, our current business culture quietly turns a blind eye to all the ways we cheat our customers through price gouging. We cheat our employees out of well-deserved profit-sharing and health benefits, our partners by holding our cards close to our chest, and by taking credit for work that is not our own. These are just a few examples that we have all likely experienced at some point in our careers. I dare say, we steal from each other in a thousand different ways on a thousand different days. The current rules of business today reward the sneakiest, the shrewdest and the ones who can get away with it. Once we name it for what it really is, "lies," we can no longer bury our heads in the sand and separate our personal from our professional behavior.

Stealing comes from a place of lack or want. When we understand this essence, we are more apt to understand the ways this creeps into our business. We can lack brand awareness, customer attention, traction, engagement, customer loyalty, and even respect. In every area where there is perception of lack or actual shortage of resources, there is an opportunity for growth if we apply the right antidote.

The antidote to stealing is giving—we must understand that reciprocity and finding mutual value is the path to creating balanced and beneficial relationships. My personal motto for all business relationships is to give more than I take and to be clear about what I hope to receive from the relationship. It sounds like this: "I'd like to tell the story of how you and/or your product solves this problem. You have an engaged audience that I'd like to gain access to. I have a product/service that could help with this need of yours. How can we work together so that everyone wins?" This direct, honest approach sets clear expectations, eliminates the need for the cat and mouse chase and the sneaky game of shells. It also allows all parties to express their business need to find common alignment.

We can give to our customers in the form of free product training and education, special offers to encourage trials, and through information they would not otherwise have access to. We can give our partners and vendors credit for solving their piece of the problem, thereby creating connective value-driven narratives. We can give back to the communities where we work, which creates goodwill and brand awareness. The list goes on and on and if we are creative and honest with our self-reflection, we can create beautiful goodness loops where everyone wins. We'll dig deeper into this later.

JOURNAL PROMPTS

1. What are the areas of my business where there is perceived lack?
2. Is integrity a core value? How do I demonstrate this daily?
3. How do I reward truth and honesty as a culture?
4. What am I stealing from?
5. How can I give back to the places I take from?

MEDITATION

Come to a quiet, seated pose. Exhale down your spine and imagine a root digging deeply into the earth. Anchor this root and imagine sister roots stretching far and wide under the dirt. Inhale deeply and find extra length in your spine, reaching tall through the crown. Bring into your awareness the areas of business that feel misaligned or lacking. Allow your intuition to guide you to see through any blocks about how your business may be misaligned with your values or lacking in some capacity. Once you have named these areas, intentionally release them and visualize what this would look and feel like if brought into balance.

Return to your breath and feel the air entering and leaving your nose. Slowly blink your eyes open. Journal whatever images came to your awareness.

INTENTIONAL AFFIRMATION

My business is abundant and generous.

"Thankfulness is the beginning of gratitude. Gratitude is the completion of thankfulness. Thankfulness may consist merely of words. Gratitude is shown in acts."

—HENRI FREDERIC AMIEL

BRAHMACHARYA

Brahmacharya is often understood as celibacy or abstinence, but for our purposes, we will discuss as it relates to non-excess or restraint. According to Deborah Adele, in her book, [1]*The Yamas and Niyamas, Exploring Yogic Ethical Practice,* "Brahmacharya literally means, 'walking with God' and invites us into the awareness of the sacredness of all life. This guideline is a call to leave greed and excess behind and walk in this world with wonder and awe, practicing non-excess and attending to each moment as holy."

Wow. We are a culture of excess. Our entire capitalistic mindset is designed to encourage excess and consumption. Our venture capital model celebrates the 10x growth model and unrestrained growth. Success is equated with excess in all its material forms. Our businesses are bloated with larger-than-necessary office spaces, our storage units are crammed with stuff we will likely never comb through, and our daily lives are filled with noise from our devices, our televisions, the media, and on and on.

In our modern world, we are constantly bombarded with information. The message of the day is to do more and be more. *More, more, more.* Yet the small whisper of our internal voice asks and yearns for less, yearns for *balance*. When I need to get work done, I have to remove myself from the chaos and self

---

[1]The Yamas and Niyamas, Exploring Yogic Ethical Practice, by Deborah Adele

isolate to get away from it all so I can focus. We push ourselves into exhaustion and many suffer from adrenal fatigue.

So what is the wisdom of incorporating brahmacharya in our businesses? The term "lifestyle business" isn't quite a dirty word, but it certainly doesn't get the same interest or carry the same clout as a tech play with the potential to return huge investments. Therefore, lifestyle businesses don't receive nearly the amount of seed money and funding that is funneled elsewhere. Although this doesn't seem like a huge deal on the surface, its implications are creating huge barriers to entry for hopeful entrepreneurs who never get a chance to bring their unique offering to market. We wind up with a homogenous business community funding projects that all look and feel the same. When we pull from the same pot, we wind up competing for the same type of talent and draw from the same well. We miss out on the benefits of small, local businesses, which shape and color the communities they serve and are the very fabric of our culture. This gap between the big box companies and small local businesses was on full display during the global pandemic. A colossal disruption in the supply chain and staffing issues forced many small businesses to close their doors, while the large players thrived. Survival of the fittest? Better optimization and resiliency? Or is the biggest wake up call for the business and entrepreneurial community that we have an imbalance of resources that only benefit a few? I do not have the answers to these questions but the conversation needs to be had.

How do we collectively better serve and protect the heart and soul of small business? How dow we shift our mindset from big to balanced? The common argument with companies like Amazon, of which I'm a loyal customer, is that it supports and gives distribution to numerous small and medium sized businesses behind the scenes. This is both true and valid yet the risk of this model is the loss of connection of these businesses to the communities and people they serve within the community. We become removed from the human who purchases the goods or services which trickles down to a less customer obsessed, do what's right for the people we serve mentality, into a reduction of mere dollars. We lose our good sense to make more cents. This disconnection is often how greed creeps into an initial healthy business environment.

Incorporating the practice of gratitude into your business model brings a layer of intention to combat excess. Learning to acknowledge daily wins, rewarding and sharing profits with employees for work well done, and honoring loyal customers and partners counters the insatiable appetite of the growth machine. We can take a hard look at the spaces our business occupies and ask if we have more than we need. Our excesses can be creative opportunities to give back, create goodness loops, and fill holes of lack in other places. The key is our understanding that having more doesn't mean feeling more. The weight of too much is a heavy burden to carry and will eventually create bloat and blight that can dampen the light of the original vision for the business.

JOURNAL PROMPTS

1. What are the areas of my business where we have excess?
2. What can we get rid of to lighten our load?
3. Are employees overworked? What is their overall state of being?
4. Who could benefit from the extra that we have to share?

MEDITATION

Come to a quiet, seated pose. Exhale down your spine and imagine a root digging deeply into the earth. Anchor this root and imagine sister roots stretching far and wide under the dirt. Inhale deeply and find extra length in your spine, reaching tall through the crown. Bring into your awareness the areas of business that feel heavy and weigh you down. Name them and shape them with your mind's eye clearly. Take each of these burdens and place them in a basket attached to a beautiful balloon. Imagine breathing into the balloon until it lifts and carries the burden away. Repeat with each item until you have released them all and have a sense of lightness and balance.

Return to your breath and feel the air entering and leaving your nose. Slowly blink your eyes open. Journal whatever images came to your awareness.

INTENTIONAL AFFIRMATION

My business is balanced and light.

"We are what we think. All that we are arises with our thoughts. With our thoughts, we make the world."

—BUDDHA

APARIGRAHA

Aparigraha is best understood as non-attachment. This can also be described as non-greed and the willingness to let things go. In business, it is easy to become attached to outcomes as the very nature of building is to hit goals, reach milestones and key performance indicators. I'm not suggesting in any way that we should discard these best practices of identifying goals and measuring our effectiveness against them. Aparigraha suggests that we do the work for the sake of doing the work so that we can bring our whole, full Selves to the table. An example of this in action is something I've witnessed time and time again. The leadership identifies key metrics for the team and these metrics are thrown up on a daily chart or dashboard and become the core focus of the effort. What ends up happening over time is that we lose the essence of why those goals are in place, and we become attached to the number.

When we become attached to numbers without the context or the soul of what and why we have these particular standards, it's easier to give permission to the "by any means necessary" voice that doesn't take into account the humanity or the connection to the people behind the goals. We send the spammy email in hopes to get the clicks. We cut corners to hit deadlines. We push products that aren't ready to be shipped. We over promise and under deliver. Most importantly, when we put the blinders of attachment on, we lose our ability to look for other opportunities and possibilities. There is a fine line between staying focused yet nimble enough for the business to find and fulfill its most valuable role for the greatest good.

For most entrepreneurs, it's a challenge to let things go. We are natural builders, visionaries and executors and this level of control is one of the reasons we are successful. But, when we hold on to outcomes too tightly, we are actually expressing fear. The antidote to fear is trust. When we incorporate bone deep trust in the Universe as a co-creator, in employees and collaborators, we create the space needed for others to stretch their wings. We begin to understand that the business will unfold as it should when we apply action and focus. I've interviewed hundreds of successful entrepreneurs over the years. Some will say their success was a combination of being in the right place at the right time, a bit of luck, grit and unwillingness to give up. Others will say they had a vision and they just knew they had to do it. What seemed to be propelling them to action was this trust, both in themselves and something bigger and more expansive than their material self.

Generosity also plays a huge role in understanding aparigraha. As businesses, we can be generous with our employees through competitive compensation packages. We can be generous with our customers with savings bundles, training and a willingness to offer excellence and legitimate problem solving. We can be generous with our local communities by offering our spaces for non-profit use, by giving back to relevant causes our business touches and much more. We can embed the notion of conscious capitalism into the very framework of our businesses so we keep energy flowing in and letting go of that which no longer serves the highest good for all involved.

JOURNAL PROMPTS

1. What are the areas of my business that I hold close to the chest?
2. What am I unwilling to let go of?
3. What outcomes am I attached to?
4. What areas of the business do I trust? What areas do I fear?
5. Where are there opportunities to be more generous?

MEDITATION

Come to a quiet, seated pose. Exhale down your spine and imagine a root digging deeply into the earth. Anchor this root and imagine sister roots stretching far and wide under the dirt. Inhale deeply and find extra length in your spine, reaching tall through the crown. Bring into your awareness the areas of business that you have become attached to. Name them and shape them with your mind's eye clearly. Take each of these attachments and place them in a flowing river and let them go. Repeat with each attachment until you have a sense of freedom.

Return to your breath and feel the air entering and leaving your nose. Slowly blink your eyes open. Journal whatever images came to your awareness.

INTENTIONAL AFFIRMATION

I let go that which no longer serves the highest good.

Incorporating the yamas in your business foundation invites us to have thoughtful, mature, relationships with each other. Considering that we are all complicated humans trying to wrangle through our individual life lessons, often fumbling and tripping over ourselves, the yamas start a conversation about how we can be more intentional together.

AHIMSA	Non-harming	Life-giving, kindness, compassion
SATYA	Truthfulness	Courage
ASTEYA	Non-stealing	Generosity
BRAHMACHARYA	Non-excess	Gratitude
APARIGRAHA	Non-attachment	Letting go, trust

"Until you make the unconscious conscious, it will direct your life and you will call it fate."

— C.G. JUNG

THE NIYAMAS

Whereas the yamas are guideposts to help us better relate to each other, human to human, the niyamas are an invitation for self development, exploration, and growth. All of which are critical if we want to create relevant, thriving, intentional businesses. The niyamas ask us to dig deeper into ourselves, to question everything and to become a forever student of the ever-evolving self. This keen introspection will help us keep our thumbs on the collective pulse since we will be in a state of presence and receptivity.

"*I will* not let anyone walk through my mind with their dirty feet."

MAHATMA GANDHI

SAUCHA

The first niyama is saucha, or purity. Saucha invites us to clean up our diet and provide the nutrients our body needs to create, to clean up our thoughts so we aren't distracted by chaos that doesn't serve our ideals, and to clean up our physical environments so we are able to focus.

When we think of self-care rituals of bathing and maintaining a clean and professional appearance, it feels like table stakes. We've been taught from the earliest age that first impressions are lasting impressions and to put our best foot forward. We do this with our physical appearances. In a distracted world, where people make instantaneous decisions about your merit and worth based on how you look, we can quickly understand why we've apparently mastered cleanliness. However, it's much more than just having clean hair, a pressed shirt and polished shoes.

Saucha invites us to be clean on the inside too. To remember that our food choices will fuel our energy. We need clean energy to create from our highest selves, yet we pack our company cupboards with chips and garbage food that diminish our energy. When we shift our understanding of our bodies as a vessel which houses a soul, we begin to see the importance of making healthier choices. Our businesses are reflections of the people who build within its confines. Healthier bodies and minds create pure environments for creativity and inspiration to flow.

Saucha asks us to be pure with our thoughts and our words. The first agreement in Don Miguel Ruiz' book, *The Four Agreements*, discusses the value and importance of being impeccable with our words. Since our words become the power we create with, it's critical to understand why it matters to honor this principle. Being clean and clear in thought, word and deed is the basis for happiness, yet is much easier to align in principle than in practice. However, knowing the wisdom behind the words will help create a pathway to better businesses aligned with our highest good.

As a marketer, I have played my role in the chaos and noise of our modern day. We are constantly being bombarded by ads and retargeted ads and messages about how this and that will make us stronger, better and faster. It's too much. As much as I love my iPhone, it has single-handedly created the most chaos, clutter and noise. All the apps I have to organize my time, to better manage my tasks, are constantly pinging me and taking my attention from true, intentional focus. We need true, intentional focus to create things. With Slack, text, email, social media, and all the things, our lives are far from pure.

I struggle with this chaos as much as the next person but am learning to build in time for myself and my team to retreat, to shut off phones and emails without fear of missing anything important. We've become so programmed that we are going to miss something that we've created an "always-on" culture that keeps us busy and leaves no room for inspiration. The root of inspiration is in-spirit. We need to create intentional, pure environments devoid of chaos and clutter, that allow our internal whisper of inspiration to come to the surface. We are invited to be clean with our thoughts and our intention so we can see clearly and proceed with purpose. Saucha and an understanding of its importance is a practice that will encourage innovation.

JOURNAL PROMPTS

1. Does my diet fuel my best self? Is the food we serve to our employees clean and nutritious?
2. What media do I consume on a daily basis? Does it cloud my creation?
3. What does my physical environment look like?
4. What are our policies around digital detoxing and retreat?

MEDITATION

Come to a quiet, seated pose. Exhale down your spine and imagine a root digging deeply into the earth. Anchor this root and imagine sister roots stretching far and wide under the dirt. Inhale deeply and find extra length in your spine, reaching tall through the crown. Bring into your awareness the areas of business that require cleaning. Name them and shape them in your mind's eye clearly. Slowly and carefully begin to clean each item with care, removing any debris, dirt and dark spots. Repeat with each attachment until you have a sense of purity.

Return to your breath and feel the air entering and leaving your nose. Slowly blink your eyes open. Journal whatever images came to your awareness.

INTENTIONAL AFFIRMATION

I am pure in thought, word and deed. My business is a reflection of this purity.

"People in the West are always getting ready to live."

–CHINESE PROVERB

SANTOSHA

The next niyama is santosha, or contentment, and boy do we have some work to do on this one. Our current culture creates a never enough mentality. We created BHAGs (big hairy audacious goals) expecting to hit them. We push ourselves and change the goal line in the middle of our races if it looks like we may win. We are always striving, always longing for more, and missing all the good stuff in the moment. Contentment and allowing others the space to feel content about their work is a company culture pearl.

It's no surprise that a 2019 Oxford University survey finally confirmed that indeed happy people are more productive. It's also a fairly accepted fact that most people do not get personal fulfillment from their work. Yet, we spend most of our best, waking hours at the very place that drains our soul tank. There is so much room for improvement to ponder how we can create business environments that support the entire individual and celebrate the here and now.

What happens in our businesses when we look inward for fulfillment, instead of always chasing the next big thing outside of ourselves? This reminds me of the book called *The Blue Ocean Strategy* by Renée Mauborgne and W. Chan Kim. In the book it describes that most businesses are swimming in crowded, red oceans fighting for the same customers, the same dollars, the same attention. The authors ask us to think outside of the chum-filled waters, farther from the chaos to where others are not yet swimming in, the big blue ocean. Contentment isn't settling for what is, but rather a deep and profound understanding and acceptance that you are exactly where you need to be. Our eyes are on our own prize; we are focused and present enough to get there.

JOURNAL PROMPTS

1. What am I discontented with?
2. How do I feel discontent in my body?
3. Is there a way to invite gratitude into my business model?

MEDITATION

Come to a quiet, seated pose. Exhale down your spine and imagine a root digging deeply into the earth. Anchor this root and imagine sister roots stretching far and wide under the dirt. Inhale deeply and find extra length in your spine, reaching tall through the crown. Bring into your awareness the areas of business that feel unsettled. Name them and shape them. Allow the root of the discontent to be exposed. Pay attention to any symbols that may arise to help better understand the dis-ease. When you're ready, express gratitude for this information and release whatever negativity you may feel. Incorporate a mantra saying, I now wish to vibrate at the frequency of gratitude. Repeat this out loud three times and notice any shifts in your body.

Return to your breath and feel the air entering and leaving your nose. Slowly blink your eyes open. Journal whatever images came to your awareness.

INTENTIONAL AFFIRMATION

I trust that things are as they should be.

"There may be a great fire in our soul, yet no one ever comes to warm himself at it, and the passers-by see only a wisp of smoke."

-VINCENT VAN GOGH

TAPAS

Tapas literally means "heat" and is often understood as self-discipline, action, and transformation. This niyama seems to squarely align with the effort required to launch, build, and sustain businesses. Anyone who has ever jumped into the entrepreneurial fire will share their numerous tales of getting burned in the process.

In her book, *The Yamas & Niyamas: Exploring Yoga's Ethical Principles*, Deborah Adele describes the essence of tapas perfectly. "Tapas can take us to the place where all of our resources are used up, where there is nothing left but weakness, where all of our so-called 'props' have been taken away. It is in this barren pace, where we have exhausted all that we have and all that we are, that new strength is shaped and character is born if we choose to fearlessly open ourselves to the experience." Tapas is the grit that spins our metaphoric rocks in the tumbler that polishes us and makes us shiny. Tapas is the fire that burns the forest so that new, lush growth can emerge from ash. Tapas is our self-disciple to stay the course, to show up when we want to hide, to pick ourselves up and put ourselves back in the ring again and again, to own our mistakes and, most importantly, to learn humbly from it all. Tapas is the not so secret ingredient for thriving intentional businesses. We must do the work. If it was easy, then everyone would do it.

Oftentimes, as we step into entrepreneurialism, we step into our true selves, as leaders, as risk-takers, and visionaries. We stop "working for the man" and build the businesses, products, and services that we wish had existed. We're driven by making things better and this passion, the heat for change, is tapas showing up in our lives. The phoenix teaches us that in order to rise, we often have to burn our lives to the ground to rise from the ashes brighter, smarter, and more equipped because of the lessons learned through the burning. We use the metaphor of burning through something when we are creating because we unconsciously understand the power of heat. We must remember and cultivate our inner flames, burn what we must, if we wish to truly transform ourselves and the business we create.

JOURNAL PROMPTS

1. Where does tapas show up in my business?
2. What daily rituals do I do to cultivate tapas?
3. What areas of my business am I most passionate about?
4. How do I handle tense and hot moments in business?
5. What do I wish to transform?

MEDITATION

Come to a quiet, seated pose. Exhale down your spine and imagine a root digging deeply into the earth. Anchor this root and imagine sister roots stretching far and wide under the dirt. Inhale deeply, reaching tall through the crown, and find extra length in your spine. Bring your attention to your heart center. Imagine a flame flickering in your chest. With each inhale, visualize the flame growing brighter and brighter until your entire body is wrapped in fire. Imagine this fire fuels your effort and creates the abundant energies you need to build.

Return to your breath and feel the air entering and leaving your nose. Slowly blink your eyes open. Journal whatever images came to your awareness.

INTENTIONAL AFFIRMATION

I have abundant energy to burn brightly.

"Knowing yourself is the beginning of all wisdom."

-ARISTOTLE

SVADHYAYA

The next niyama is svadhyaya, or self-study. Svadhyaya invites us to become the active witness of our lives and we do this by unpacking all the baggage we've brought along with us. There is big "Self" study and little "self" study and they are equally important to creating businesses aligned with our soul's purpose.

Big "S" self study is aligned with meditation, with active listening to our quiet inner voice. Big "S" study is about remembering that we are souls living out our days through the vehicle of our bodies and the engines of our minds. It's about cutting through the illusion that we are somehow separate or disconnected from everything else. That we have the ability to actually remove ourselves from the whole. Big "S" study can be guided and taught through yoga, breathing exercises, meditation practices, austerity, and numerous other spiritual and ritual practices, but the work is our own. Little "s" self-study is about digging into your shadow self. The parts of you that are hidden from others, your shame, your guilt, your fears, your attachments, and all the ways your ego tries to trick you into thinking you're much smaller than you truly are.

This work is not about fixing your broken parts; rather, it's about remembering who you are and what you were put on this earth to do. We just need to clear the path of debris so we can actually find our way. We all have paths littered with garbage, we all have work to do. We all must unpack our limiting belief systems that are usually wrapped in language as "shoulds," "musts," "always-es," and "nevers."

Debora Adele tells the story of when Yogiraj Achala took his young son to the Mississippi River. "The son, looking into the river, asked his dad if the river was polluted. Yogiraj responded that no, the river is only carrying the pollution, the river itself is pure. Our minds are like the river carrying things in it. If we identify with what the mind is carrying—thoughts, stories, beliefs—then we will think we are those things. However, if we identify with the Divine within us (the pure river) and merely watch the thoughts float by, we will know we are simply carrying the thoughts, stories and belief; they *are not* who we are."

How does self-study apply to business? It makes us better, more compassionate, humble, curious people when we realize that every soul on the planet is doing really hard work to re-member.

Re-membering is diving deep into our big and little selves to figure out what we are here to learn and how we can best contribute when we show up as our actualized, whole selves. Being a good human is good for business. Period.

JOURNAL PROMPTS

1. Make a list of the areas in your life where I should, must, always, and never.
2. Without thinking, make a list of the first 5 things that come to mind that describes my business as it is now? (Hint, your answers will give you clues about what is inside you since our businesses are macro reflections of ourselves.)
3. How can I become the witness of my life?
4. What type of meditation practice is most appealing? Walks in nature, on the beach, yoga, guided meditation?
5. What books would I like to read to help facilitate my re-membering? If you're unsure, please visit our website for our readers list.

MEDITATION

Come to a quiet, seated pose. Exhale down your spine and imagine a root digging deeply into the earth. Anchor this root and imagine sister roots stretching far and wide under the dirt. Inhale deeply, reaching tall through the crown, and find extra length in your spine. Bring your attention to your heart center and begin to imagine breathing from your heart to your mind. Ask the question, who am I?

Return to your breath and feel the air entering and leaving your nose. Slowly blink your eyes open. Journal whatever images came to your awareness.

INTENTIONAL AFFIRMATION

I Am That. That I Am.

"If you surrender to the wind, you can ride it."

—ANONYMOUS

ISHVARA PRANIDHANA

Finally, the niyamas end with Ishavara Pranidhana, otherwise known as surrender. When it's all said and done, and we've done the work and pushed the rocks, and dived into our shadows, and basked in the Light, we must acknowledge that there is a Divine force at work within all of our lives and reflected in our businesses. We call this a million different names: God, Goddess, Nature, the Universe, Fate, Grace, Luck, Timing, and it is alive and flowing through us whether we acknowledge it or not.

Artists call it the flow and when we can let go enough to let the wind move through us, we create magic. Opening yourself and creating space for the flow is when we get to rise in our sovereignty and move into the role of co-creator of our lives and businesses. We can carve out space to limit distractions and eliminate disruptions. When we can value the precious power of trust and faith and its role in business, we will create entities that are enriching, fulfilling, generous, kind, honest, steadfast, productive, and yes, even prosperous.

JOURNAL PROMPTS

1. What does the word surrender mean to me?
2. Where can I surrender in my business life?
3. Describe a time I experienced the flow.
4. How can I create a structure that supports the flow?
5. How do I perceive the Divine?

MEDITATION

Come to a quiet, seated pose. Exhale down your spine and imagine a root digging deeply into the earth. Anchor this root and imagine sister roots stretching far and wide under the dirt. Inhale deeply, reaching tall through the crown, and find extra length in your spine. Bring your attention to your heart center and begin to imagine breathing from your heart to your third eye, the space between your brow. Ask the question, "What is my purpose?"

Return to your breath and feel the air entering and leaving your nose. Slowly blink your eyes open. Journal whatever images came to your awareness.

INTENTIONAL AFFIRMATION

I trust the Universe flows through me. I allow this energy to transform my business for the greatest good.

Doing the hard work of discovering who you are, and building a business structure aligned with creating space for your employees and partners to also do this work, is a revolutionary idea. We aren't mixing religion with business. We're honoring the spirit in each of us, and inviting our Big Selves to the table. With self awareness, we will be able to more clearly see how our little selves color our vision and we will be able to see and help others see more clearly. Isn't that the very definition of a visionary?

SAUCHA	Purity in appearance, thought, words and action
SANTOSHA	Contentment
TAPAS	Heat, passion, action
SVADHYAYA	Self-study, reflection, contemplation
ISHVARA PRANIDHANA	Surrender

"The power of intention is the power to manifest, to create, to live a life of unlimited abundance, and to attract into your life the right people at the right moments."

-WAYNE DWYER

THE POWER OF INTENTION

According to [2]Merriam-Webster's dictionary, the definition of intention is 1a : what one intends to do or bring about. b : the object for which a prayer, mass, or pious act is offered. 2 : a determination to act in a certain way : resolve. 3 intentions plural : purpose with respect to marriage.

Or the [3]vocabulary.com definition is "An intention is an idea that you plan (or intend) to carry out. If you mean something, it's an intention. Your goal, purpose, or aim is your intention. It's something you mean to do, whether you pull it off or not.

It's important to start with these definitions because we likely have a basic understanding of what an intention is but need an extra point of reference for clarity. When we talk about intention, we are getting into the realm of spiritualism whether we realize it or not. The heart of intention is understanding our power to create.

---

[2] Merriam-Webster

[3] vocabulary.com search

Most businesses have goals, purposes, and aims, so it's no surprise that our intentions are part of this equation. Yet, if we think more broadly about our ability to manifest what we imagine and intend to bring about, we can harness the power of a focused mind and can push beyond limitations defined by our understanding of the five senses. Common sense thinking and problem solving leverages our 'common senses' of sight, sound, taste, touch, and smell but do not include our abilities to create with our minds. A well-known quote from Mahatma Gandhi states, "Your beliefs become your thoughts. Your thoughts become your words. Your words become your actions. Your actions become your habits. Your habits become your values. Your values become your destiny."

We can learn to harness the monkey mind and create true focus. When we do so, we can begin to create with intention.
As discussed in the previous chapter that briefly describes yama and niyama, the first two limbs of Patanjali's eight-limbed path, we have to master the foundation of right living with both ourselves and others. Patanjali makes it quite clear in the yoga sutras that you must master these restraints and observances before we can truly master the mind. "Without cultivating the yamas and niyamas, the mind will not manifest the requisite state of sattva (purity) without which there can be no meditation and thus no practice of yoga…"

This relates to creating an intentional business because we and our employees and our colleagues are distracted. Our addiction to the pings and reminders and notifications we receive on our phones have created cluttered, chaotic minds. We ask these same cluttered, chaotic minds to create, to solve problems, and to show up to do our best work. But there is a massive disconnect because we as a collective culture are sick and have dis-ease, an abandonment of ease. This greatly hinders the critical focus required to do in-spired (in-spirited) work and quite frankly costs organizations a ton of money through wasted time, dullness, and mistakes.

This race to the bottom can be resolved if we can find our center and restore balance through focus. We have literally taken the soul out of business while Darwin's survival of the fittest mentality has put the individual over the collective. We do not have to be defined by our current condition of competition and can learn to cooperate, collaborate, and connect. Unrestrained competition can create fear and we all know that fear can crush creativity and innovation. We can incorporate wisdom into our corporations and create a new way of doing business.

JOURNAL PROMPTS

1. What does intention mean to me?
2. How are my business goals or intentions communicated within the organization?
3. What are my limited "common sense" beliefs?
4. How has distraction affected my progress?
5. Where does fear lurk in my business? What intentional changes can I make to combat this?

MEDITATION

Come to a quiet, seated pose. Exhale down your spine and imagine a root digging deeply into the earth. Anchor this root and imagine sister roots stretching far and wide under the dirt. Inhale deeply and find extra length in your spine, reaching tall through the crown.

Begin to connect with your breath and feel the air entering and leaving your nose. Begin to relax your face and unclench your jaw as you begin to relax all of your muscles. Once you begin to soften in your body, bring your awareness to the space between your brows. Ask yourself to bring into your awareness any limiting beliefs that are holding you back. Allow whatever mental imagery to arise without judgement, name what you see. Once you have a clear image in your mind, relax your body even further, and breathe intentionally into this image, blowing it out of your mind and releasing it into the world. Slowly bring the equal and opposite of the limiting belief into your mind screen.

So if you see fear, imagine courage. If you see weakness, imagine strength. Name and claim this equal and opposite belief and begin to transform the limiting belief into its empowered polar opposite. Notice any shifts in your body and breathing.

Return to your natural breath and feel the air entering and leaving your nose. Slowly blink your eyes open. Journal whatever images came to your awareness. Give gratitude for this insight.

INTENTIONAL AFFIRMATION

My business is a reflection of my soul's purpose.

CLARITY THROUGH CONCENTRATION

There are numerous ways to increase our ability to concentrate. Patanjali outlines the following limbs to assist this aim.

Asanas, the third limb, are the yogic postures. My teacher often mentions the purpose of asana is to prepare the body to sit in meditation without distraction. These poses help move energy or chi throughout the body to create optimal health. Through the practice of asana, we develop the discipline required for concentration.

Pranayama is the fourth limb and is generally understood to be breath work. When we bring our awareness to our breath and learn to control the inhalations and exhalations, we begin to strengthen our nervous systems and wrangle the monkey mind. Practicing various breathing techniques connects our body, mind, and breath and is one of the fastest ways to learn or remember how to focus.

Pratyhara is the fifth limb and essentially means withdrawal of the senses; we eliminate any possible distractions and begin to direct our attention inward. Most of us show up in this world like light bulbs, our light is diffused and splayed. But learning to draw our senses inward teaches us to project our energy like a laser beam, which is so much more powerful. Pratyhara in combination with the sixth limb, dharana, or single pointed concentration, is where the heavy lifting of yoga training happens and is a precursor to a true meditation practice.

In our Western world, many have dismissed the idea of incorporating meditation into their daily ritual because they have tried to sit cross-legged and seemingly failed. However, there are preparations and steps needed in order to have a positive meditation experience.

Dhyana, the seventh limb of yoga, is what most Westerners consider meditation. It's the process of inward contemplation. We quiet the mind and try to create and hold stillness. This is no easy task but strengthening the practice through the work in the earlier limbs prepares the mind for uninterrupted focus and concentration. When we are able to hold this state of stillness, we can achieve the eighth limb, which is called Samadhi, understood as ecstasy. We are able to re-member our Unity with all that is in a perfect state of harmony and bliss.

We can be intentional about regaining our power and focus with the antidote of a consistent yoga practice. Offering yoga instruction and implementing yoga into the work day is far more valuable than an employee perk. It could very well be the conditioning that creates the conditions for true innovation.

JOURNAL PROMPTS

1. What is my experience with yoga?
2. How has my perception changed when I learned that yoga is more than postures alone?
3. How can I eliminate distractions in my business?
4. What are the potential benefits of improved concentration?
5. How can yoga be incorporated in my business?

MEDITATION

Come to a quiet, seated pose. Exhale down your spine and imagine a root digging deeply into the earth. Anchor this root and imagine sister roots stretching far and wide under the dirt. Inhale deeply and find extra length in your spine, reaching tall through the crown.

Begin to connect with your breath and feel the air entering and leaving your nose. Begin to relax your face and unclench your jaw as you begin to relax all of your muscles. Once you begin to soften in your body, bring your awareness to the space between your brows. Count down from the number 13, taking a moment to pause and hold the visual number in your mind. Notice the mind and your ability or inability to remain focused on the number. Practice this again and again until you are able to complete the cycle with mental distraction or interruption. Continue this meditation by repeating this cycle. Notice when your mind begins to shift and resume the count.

Return to your natural breath and feel the air entering and leaving your nose. Slowly blink your eyes open. Journal whatever images came to your awareness. Give gratitude for this insight. Repeat daily to strengthen your ability to focus.

INTENTIONAL AFFIRMATION

I am focused and clear. My business is focused and clear.

THE FIVE PS CHECKLIST

Over the years, I've interviewed hundreds of successful entrepreneurs. However, recently I've noticed a fascinating trend with the women I've met. Many have multiple revenue streams and have their hands in numerous projects. They carry numerous titles that reflect their different roles so it's difficult to pin down "what" they do. This rings true for me, and I find that I choose projects that fulfill different aspects of my personality which keeps me sharp and engaged. We are complex beings and the gig economy, the ability to find short-term, contract work aligned with numerous passions on-demand, has paved the way so that we can create livelihood from nontraditional ways. We can create intentional businesses if we consider the following five Ps.

PURPOSE

It all starts with purpose. This is the very reason why the business exists. We set our intentions to achieve our purpose. When we don't have a clear and articulated purpose for being, it's nearly impossible to have an impact. We need a beacon of purpose to guide decision-making about which direction to take, which products to build, which verticals to explore. It's no surprise that purpose is connected to the word intention as it relates to marriage. Marriages are unions and commitments between people. What if we felt a sense of unity and commitment to the relationship with our business? Knowing the purpose (and your purpose as an entrepreneur) is mission critical.

PAYCHECK

We know fear cuts the flow of creativity. For many of us, the fear of not being able to provide for ourselves and our families is on the top of our list. I've learned this the hard way by jumping into business creation without a plan for being paid, assuming that, "If I build it they will come." Not true. While we are in business creation mode and ideation, we have to consider where the paycheck will come from. The gig economy has created opportunities to wear many hats but ideally, we find alignment between what we are building and how we get paid so we can leverage synergies and preserve the energy needed to build.

PARTNERSHIPS

Our intentional businesses need collaborators. Partnerships not only allow for more comprehensive solutions but they also give us access to new people. When we ditch the dated Darwin mentality and build on the concept of knowing that we are truly better together, we can find partnerships that fill our gaps, amplify our values, and connect new opportunities. Remember the guild when thinking about which partnerships will be fruitful.

PASSION

Building businesses is not for the faint of heart. Every time I begin with a new start-up, I'm reminded of how difficult it actually is to gain traction and momentum. Passion has to come into play or it will be easy to duck out when things get uncomfortable. Most people fulfill passion projects on the side, but that draws our energies away from our business. So find a way to put what you care deeply about into your mission so you can keep your flames burning bright.

POWER

We step into our personal power when we are clear, focused, and intentional. We are able to draw from a deep well of courage, wisdom, and intuition when our business reflects our values and vision. Our outer world reflects what's happening in our inner world so we can take this information, own it, and with intention transform our businesses to reflect our deepest desires.

JOURNAL PROMPTS:

1. What is the purpose of my business?
2. How do I get paid?
3. Who is my ideal partner?
4. What is my passion? How can I incorporate this into my business?
5. When do I feel most powerful?

MEDITATION

Come to a quiet, seated pose. Exhale down your spine and imagine a root digging deeply into the earth. Anchor this root and imagine sister roots stretching far and wide under the dirt. Inhale deeply and find extra length in your spine, reaching tall through the crown.

Begin to connect with your breath and feel the air entering and leaving your nose. Begin to relax your face and unclench your jaw as you begin to relax all of your muscles. Once you begin to soften in your body, bring your awareness to the space between your brows. Ask yourself to bring into your awareness your deepest desire for your business. You may wish to add a mantra to be repeated three times, "I now wish to vibrate at the frequency of clarity" to assist this meditation. Allow whatever mental imagery to surface without judgement.

Return to your natural breath and feel the air entering and leaving your nose. Slowly blink your eyes open. Journal whatever images came to your awareness. Give gratitude for this insight.

INTENTIONAL AFFIRMATION

I reclaim my power. My business supports my deepest desires.

"You reclaim your power by loving what you were once taught to hate."

BRYANT H. MCGILL

GET OFF YOUR BACK

Now more than ever, we need to learn to trust and cultivate our intuition, our inner knowing. When I was pregnant with my first child, I attended all the birthing classes, read all the books, watched all the movies, and learned what I could to prepare myself for my son's arrival. When the time came, I checked into the hospital and the flurry of nurses and doctors took over. I was told to lay on my back, was hooked up to machines, had an epidural that took away my ability to connect with the intelligence of my body and the signals it was designed to send. It was a disaster and it nearly killed me.

When my second child was born, I took control and listened to my intuition and my body and got off my back so I could use the tools I had access to, including gravity. The whole thing went much more smoothly so by the time my third child was born, I trusted myself enough to know what I was capable of. We hand over our power every single day to people with louder voices than ours who speak with authority. We are told to get on our backs, not because it's best for us, but because it's easier for them. Intuition is not a soft skill in business. It is an absolute superpower that should be cultivated as mission critical. Learning to trust our intuition and act accordingly is at the heart of any intentional business.

The process of learning to trust your intuition takes time. Unfortunately, the programming to conform to familial and societal structures and belief systems can strip the individual of the recognition of her own voice. We must take the time to relearn how to listen, not only to the whisper of the soul, but also to the intelligence of the body. This can come in the form of hairs rising, chest tightening, mouth drying, shivers, heat or numerous other physical cues. With the constant distraction of technology and entertainment, many of us live in a constant state of numbness and are not dialed into the physical sensations we have access to. Spending time in nature, with shoes off, connecting to earth energy is a powerful place to start. Notice how your body feels when you are not speaking your truth. What happens to your skin when you know someone else is being dishonest. Pay attention to these subtleties and cultivate the language of intuition.

JOURNAL PROMPTS

1. Describe an instance when I gave away my personal power?

2. How accurate is my intuition?

3. What could I do to strengthen my intuition?

4. What other soft skills are superpowers in business?

5. Do I trust myself?

MEDITATION

Come to a quiet, seated pose. Exhale down your spine and imagine a root digging deeply into the earth. Anchor this root and imagine sister roots stretching far and wide under the dirt. Inhale deeply and find extra length in your spine, reaching tall through the crown.

Begin to connect with your breath and feel the air entering and leaving your nose. Begin to relax your face and unclench your jaw as you begin to relax all of your muscles. Once you begin to soften in your body, bring your awareness to the space between your brows. Ask yourself to bring into your awareness a moment where you gave away your personal power. Visualize as many of the circumstances around this moment as you can possibly remember. Now visualize a redo of this moment where you remained in your power. How did the circumstances change and differ? How do you feel in this new moment? Integrate this feeling of empowered being into your body, releasing the feeling of powerlessness. Notice the changes and the shifts in your being.

Return to your natural breath and feel the air entering and leaving your nose. Slowly blink your eyes open. Journal whatever images came to your awareness. Give gratitude for this insight.

INTENTIONAL AFFIRMATION

I trust my intuition and the wisdom of my body.

"The monotony and solitude of a quiet life stimulates the creative mind."

—ALBERT EINSTEIN

INTENTIONAL QUIET

When we understand that the Universe is in constant motion (and many of us can feel this), we quickly realize the importance of rest. The very nature of waves needs the lull to force the energy to go up again and again and again. Our business culture does not honor quiet. We are a caffeinated hustle and grind, go get 'em group of exhausted, fried, and unfocused folks. Our businesses suffer because of it.

Intuitively we know that we must slow down to have the energy to speed up or we will simply run out of metaphorical gas. The analogy of our bodies as vehicles is not a bad one. We must maintain our cars so they can carry us through life experiences, and we spend hours and dollars on oil changes and new tires, but we allow ourselves to slurp coffee and grab an energy bar to maintain our momentum. This must stop.

Meditation spaces, contemplation pods, quarterly personal retreats, four-day work weeks, and quiet hours, all sound luxurious and lofty and non-essential. However, when we apply the wisdom and the knowledge of yoga, nature, and the laws of the Universe, we know that our current schedules are out of alignment. We are stressed, overworked, and sick. Being sick and depleted is far more expensive than investing in refueling.

We can create rituals of quiet throughout our day. The afternoon tea ceremony is a wonderful ritual that, with intention, can become a break for reflection, contemplation, and replenishment. A simple commitment for a daily walk in nature alone, without a phone, music, or friends, can begin the reconnection to ourselves. Mauna, or sacred silence, is a wonderful way to cultivate quiet. This practice has its roots in Hindu tradition and according to the Bhagavad Gita aims to not just quiet our mouths, but also our minds. This practice helps conserve vital energy and reminds us of the sacredness of quiet which most of us have felt at some point in our lives. A moment of silence can be deeply moving and have profound effects.

Being quiet and disconnecting from chaos opens up space for creativity and inspiration. When we are exhausted, we lower our vibrations and lose our ability to resonate and find our flow. If we want to be responsible co-creators as we launch new ideas, products, and services, we must value quiet so we can listen for new opportunities and allow inspiration to emerge from within.

JOURNAL PROMPTS

1. How many hours do I work a week?
2. How many hours do I spend being intentionally quiet?
3. When do my best ideas come to me?
4. Do I respect other's need for quiet time? Do I respect my own?
5. How do I feel during a moment of silence?

MEDITATION

Come to a quiet, seated pose. Exhale down your spine and imagine a root digging deeply into the earth. Anchor this root and imagine sister roots stretching far and wide under the dirt. Inhale deeply and find extra length in your spine, reaching tall through the crown.

Begin to connect with your breath and feel the air entering and leaving your nose. Begin to relax your face and unclench your jaw as you begin to relax all of your muscles. Once you begin to soften in your body, bring your awareness to the space between your brows. Notice any sounds that may surround you. Notice any sounds or noise in your own mental chatter. Focus on the sound of your own breathing in and out rhythmically. Drop into your heart and tune into the sound of its own beating rhythm. Hold your awareness at the heart center until you can easily tune into your own beat. Hold awareness at your chest, the very seat of your soul.

Return to your natural breath and feel the air entering and leaving your nose. Take three intentional breaths. One for being fully human, one for being fully divine, and one for being anthropos, an integrated being. Slowly blink your eyes open. Journal whatever images came to your awareness. Give gratitude for this insight.

INTENTIONAL AFFIRMATION
When I quiet my mind, wisdom flows through me.

"Adopt the pace of nature. Her secret is patience."

-RALPH WALDO EMERSON

NATURE'S BLUEPRINT

GET IN RHYTHM

Nature is a perfect teacher. Our daily lives are guided by the rise and setting of the sun, of the moon and her cycles, the ebb and flow of the tides, our body's circadian rhythms, and of course the cycles of the seasons. In fact, so much of our day is guided by these natural rhythms, we may take them for granted or have forgotten the importance of how these rhythms move through and around us. Understanding cycles is equally important in business.

In the past few years, I have begun studying plants to increase my knowledge of herbalism and for my tea company, Intentionaliteas. Once I started down this path, a whole world of wisdom began to unfold. Now a hobby gardener, I find great pleasure sitting and watching the plants grow, adapt, and change as the conditions change. One of the greatest lessons the natural world teaches us is about transformation. Everything at all times, is in a constant state of change. It's either growing or dying and when it dies, the compost returns to the soil to provide valuable nutrients needed to grow again. There is nothing linear about the rhythm of nature. She teaches us that all things, when we really stop and pay attention, are in a perpetual cycle, an interconnected, mutually beneficial cycle.

In business, we tend to think in a linear way of moving from A to B, to achieve certain goals. When we think in this manner we can easily miss the big picture. This is particularly relevant in business planning. It's no surprise that we break up the year in quarters, which actually align beautifully to nature's cycles of spring, summer, autumn, and winter. When we tune into the energies of each season, and align our planning with the natural energies around us, we begin to move in harmony with the rhythms of nature.

For example, spring is a wonderful time to plant seeds and prepare the beds; the earth is starting to wake up from being dormant. Rain feeds the fields and the days begin to get warmer and warmer which energizes the seeds in the soil and encourages them to grow and wake up. As humans, we've all experienced the excitement of spring fever; our bodies get excited and start to wake up. Spring is a time of planning and preparation. It's a wonderful time to do foundational work to prepare for the coming harvest of summer.

In summer, for example, the days are long and hot. The sun burns brightly and the labor of the spring can be harvested and the crop preserved to last for the remainder of the year.

The insects and the birds and growth are at their peak. The energy is high and encourages us to put in the work, to honor the sweat on our brows as we put forth the effort, enjoying the bounty of the harvest and celebrating its gifts. The summer is a time to labor, the earth is awake and is at its peak of energy and resourcefulness. It's interesting that culturally, we tend to take breaks in the summer, we vacation and hang at the beach when the natural energies are about growth, about reaping what we've sown, and bearing fruit.

As the cycle of nature shifts to autumn, the days get shorter, the nights cooler, the harvest has been picked. The leaves fall from the trees and cover the ground, and any remaining fruit will either provide nourishment for some lucky group of insects or animals, or will eventually rot and return to the soil as nutrients. Cold weather crops can be rotated in beds for the last hoorah of the growing cycle. Autumn is all about preparation. The trees begin to shed leaves so they can store energy for the coming winter. Autumn reminds us about the waning energies needed for conservation.

Then there is winter. The earth has gone to sleep, the animals have taken retreat to hibernate, things slow down to a slumber. The days are short, the darkness is long, which invites our planet to rest, to renew, to reflect. Even the snow covers the earth in a giant blanket of silvery white goodness. Our bodies yearn for cozy moments around the fire and contemplation.

Winter is a time to go inward, to process, to absorb and conserve. Yet for most, we do the exact opposite. The hustle and bustle of the holidays keep us over-scheduled, active and out of sync with nature's rhythm. Winter is a wonderful time to analyze, create space for contemplation about what worked and didn't work in the business, and to map out plans for the seasons ahead.

And then the cycles, the transformation of seasons, repeat again and again and again. We can chart them, plan for them, and prepare for what's ahead and honor the rhythm of the moment. When we become in tune with the cycles around us, we realign ourselves to the heartbeat of the earth. The rhythm of our own beating hearts, and of our own chest rising and falling with each breath, reminds us of the power of being in sync. We become sick when our breathing or our heart rate is out of rhythm. Our businesses are no different if we pause to observe the effects and notice when we are in or out of rhythm.

Another wonderful cycle to honor is that of the butterfly. The butterfly develops through a process called metamorphosis. This is a Greek word that means transformation or change in shape. It's no surprise this is a powerful metaphor for business as we strive to create something from nothing. Whenever I spend time in meditation and focus on the lessons of the butterfly, I am reminded that we are born to transform. We tend to fear pain and discomfort and resist change at every turn. The butterfly life cycle is simple: egg, caterpillar, pupa and adult. These stages cannot be bypassed or sidestepped. It's part of the process and required to move fully into the next. The caterpillar is all about feeding and making sure there is enough nourishment to provide for the growth phase of pupa. Although the pupa may appear on the outside to be stagnant and still, the changes happening on the inside are truly remarkable. This is the transitional stage of transformation when things may appear to slow down because the hard work is being done on the inside. Finally, the butterfly emerges from the chrysalis and is ready to fly. This adult stage of the life cycle is about reproduction. In the adult stage, the butterfly cannot grow. Its job is to mate and lay eggs, or in business terms, connect, collaborate and seed for the future.

The wisdom comes from understanding the stage of creation the business is in. Then, learning to honor the current cycle instead of just insisting on the grow or die mentality. This is an act of defiance against the status quote and a true test of patience.

But, nature's blueprint clearly reveals that if we want to find our wings, we must honor the cycle to get there. If you've ever spent time truly looking at the wings of a Yellow Tail Swallow, my favorite butterfly, you'll notice the beautiful bold yellow blocks of color on her wings. There are also tiny white dots that perfectly accentuate the yellow and the black stripes. You'll notice touches of pointillistic vibrant blue on the edges of the wings and a spot of orange as an unexpected surprise that could be easily missed. Every line, every shape, every color is a perfect mirror image of the other wing, a composition in balance. If our Creator takes such great care with the tiniest of details of a butterfly's wings, certainly we can give the same attention to the details of our own businesses.

We should understand that our businesses are not separate from the natural world. The unity of a collective beat creates a deeply connected, rooted base that is difficult to dislodge. Our job as entrepreneurs and business leaders is to tune into this rhythm and to honor its wisdom.

JOURNAL PROMPT

1. What is my personal daily rhythm?
2. How does this show up in my business?
3. Identify my business cycles.
4. How are my business cycles out of rhythm with nature's cycles?
5. How can I incorporate this knowledge into my planning?

MEDITATION

Come to a quiet, seated pose. Exhale down your spine and imagine a root digging deeply into the earth. Anchor this root and imagine sister roots stretching far and wide under the dirt. Inhale deeply, reaching tall through the crown, and find extra length in your spine. Bring your attention to your heart center, place your left hand gently on your heart and connect to its rhythm. Focus your awareness here, and hold this connection to your own beat.

Return to your breath and feel the air entering and leaving your nose. Slowly blink your eyes open. Journal whatever images came to your awareness.

INTENTIONAL AFFIRMATION

I am in rhythm with nature's cycles. My business is in constant transformation.

THE SEVEN GUILD MEMBERS

There is an idea in permaculture gardening called a tree guild. At its core, a guild is a community of plants working together to establish healthy, sustainable orchards. When I first read about a guild and how the elements work together to bear more fruit, I could not help draw the connections to partner collaboration and marketing.

The idea is simple. We each have a unique role to play. We have something that we do better than others, and when combined with others that do the things they are better than others at doing, we are stronger and bear more fruit. Let's face it, we can not be great at all things. The guild model reminds us that we are better together and gives us a framework for knowing who we need on our teams and what partners we might need to create intentional businesses. Let's break down the components of the guild.

There are seven key tasks or members that should be explored to ensure we are creating holistically and considering a number of possible factors while we build. The seven "jobs" in permaculture guilding are the following.

1. Attractors: Attract beneficial insects
2. Deterrents: Deter wildlife
3. Fertilizers: Fertilize and enrich the soil
4. Mulchers: Mulch the earth and preserve energy

5. Pollinators: Produce nectar to pollinate

6. Repellents: Repel pests

7. Suppressors: Suppress weeds and grass

Attractors

The attractors are your relationship-driven people. They might be your public relations or marketing mavens. Their job is to create interest and appeal to attract beneficial customers, influencers, and interest in what you're doing. This is a very specific type of person with very specific skills. They often are people-people and care deeply about doing good. Identifying who these people are and ensuring you have an attractor on your team is mission critical for early stage and growth companies. These folks know who needs to be connected and have the ability to pull them in to create the necessary exposure, partnerships, and buzz needed for mutual benefit.

Deterrents

The deterrents are the people who can see the pitfalls coming before anyone else. They are often members of the client facing team who have experience in the wild and know what's out there. They understand what can derail the business or marketing plan and are able to create a border before the entire effort is destroyed. These people may not be as fun to work with but are as important to the guild as anyone else. Any gardener knows the defeat of having unwanted wildlife eat your crop right as it was starting to flourish. We need the deterrents to keep these energies at bay.

Fertilizers

The fertilizers are the people who are checking the data and making tweaks. They are the ones who have their pulse on what is happening at any given moment and ensure the right amount of nutrients are being applied to keep things healthy. Since the wisdom of nature teaches us that change is constant, the fertilizers know to check and recheck to make sure the team has what it needs to be successful. These are your fixers and know when to course correct.

Mulchers

The mulchers are the project managers. These are the folks that help the team preserve energy. They help retain valuable resources and maintain healthy temperatures within the group. These are the peacekeepers and help ensure the team stays on track, has the correct resources, and can maintain the right amount of momentum to complete.

Pollinators

The pollinators are the product team or the folks who curate amazing products or services. These folks are responsible for creating the goods that will actually bear fruit. They understand the importance of their role in the guild because without them, without sticky, valuable, well-designed products or services, the guild will not be fruitful.

Repellants The repellents are the ones who have the big picture. They may have an understanding of what companions will keep pests away. They are able to create healthier, higher yield systems because they make everyone else better. The repellents are your leaders, your visionaries, who have a big picture of how diversity makes everything better. They repel negativity and create protection for the entire team.

Suppressors The suppressors are your human resource people. They work with the repellants to identify and weed out negativity and weeds that can choke project momentum and stifle growth. Since businesses are made of humans, we know that occasionally, teams struggle with interpersonal conflict. This happens, some personalities just don't build well together, and that's ok if we have our suppressors to minimize the impact of the unwanted weeds that will take over if allowed.

Now that we've explored the various aspects of a guild, we can apply this thinking to project teams; we can better see where we may have holes in our organization, and even apply these principles to how and whom we go to market with.

JOURNAL PROMPT

1. Identify the following people in my business?
    - Attractor:
    - Deterrent:
    - Fertilizer:
    - Mulcher:
    - Pollinator:
    - Repellant:
    - Suppressor:
2. Who am I missing in my business?
3. Where is there overlap in my business?
4. How and where can my community work better together?

MEDITATION

Come to a quiet, seated pose. Exhale down your spine and imagine a root digging deeply into the earth. Anchor this root and imagine sister roots stretching far and wide under the dirt. Inhale deeply and find extra length in your spine, reaching tall through the crown.

Begin to connect with your breath and feel the air entering and leaving your nose. Begin to relax your face and unclench your jaw as you begin to relax all of your muscles. Once you begin to soften in your body, bring your awareness to the space between your brows. Begin to imagine a thriving orchard. Notice how all parts of the community work together to support the other. What do you see? Ask how these lessons can be applied to your current situation.

Return to your breath and feel the air entering and leaving your nose. Slowly blink your eyes open. Journal whatever images came to your awareness.

INTENTIONAL AFFIRMATION

My business is whole. My team has value and purpose.

THE TREE

Many of us read the story, *The Giving Tree,* by Shel Silverstein at some point in our life. The tree gives and gives and gives to the boy she loved so well, without asking for anything in return. Although this book is sweet, it makes me feel a bit sad because it seems like the boy takes more from the tree than he returns. This idea of mutual benefit and shared value is called reciprocity. We'll take a deeper dive into reciprocity as it relates to mindful marketing. In our intentional businesses, we do not want to be the tree that just gives and gives nor do we want to be the boy who takes and takes. We want to find the balance of both giving and receiving.

Trees are the masters of balance. Deeply secure roots anchor the tree to the earth so the tree can reach and grow into maturity. Even though we cannot see the roots under the soil, they reach far and wide, sending signals and messages to other trees. These roots are like a silent underground network communicating for the common good. Strength comes from the wind. The tree adapts to its environment and actually gets stronger with difficult conditions. The wisdom for business is to grow where you're planted, to allow our surrounding conditions and constraints to fuel problem solving so we can thrive wherever we are.

The branches and leaves reach for sunlight to send to the rest of the tree so it can be converted to energy; this provides the very oxygen we need to breathe.These same leaves provide protection and shade from the sun. Trees are both food and home to furry, feathered, and tiny creatures. Nothing is wasted. What the tree no longer needs becomes repurposed as energy for more life. Trees are mystical and calming, with the gentle pulsing of branches look like a wave and soft hello as Khalil Gibran points out, "Forget not that the earth delights to feel your bare feet and the winds long to play with your hair."

The acorn, the seed of the mighty oak, represents possibility and is a symbol of hard work paying off. When an acorn falls to the earth, it is nourished and warmed by the sun, with patience and time, transforms into what it was meant to become. The tiny acorn contains everything needed to become the mighty oak, it just needs the right conditions to reach its full potential. Mighty things can come from tiny, humble beginnings.
Trees remind us of our interconnectedness. They remind us that strength comes in silence and to stand tall and take our place in the forest of others. They are useful, resourceful, and resilient. They are the silent guards and gentle reminders of the

power of being. So our businesses, when deeply rooted with attention, give more than they take. Let us weave this wisdom into our planning.

JOURNAL PROMPTS

1. Where has my business been strengthened by hardship?
2. What are my current acorns?
3. How is my business interconnected to the community?

MEDITATION

Come to a quiet, seated pose. Exhale down your spine and imagine a root digging deeply into the earth. Anchor this root and imagine sister roots stretching far and wide under the dirt. Inhale deeply and find extra length in your spine, reaching tall through the crown.

Begin to connect with your breath and feel the air entering and leaving your nose. Begin to relax your face and unclench your jaw as you begin to relax all of your muscles. Once you begin to soften in your body, bring your awareness to the space between your brows. Begin to imagine a tree. Visualize as many different aspects you can. Imagine sharing your breath with the tree and the beautiful exchange of carbon dioxide into oxygen we share. Bring into your awareness something you may be struggling with in your business. Imagine how this could be an opportunity for creative problem solving or strengthening of the situation it touches. Express gratitude for all these lessons.

Return to your breath and feel the air entering and leaving your nose. Slowly blink your eyes open. Journal whatever images came to your awareness. Give gratitude for this connection.

INTENTIONAL AFFIRMATION

My roots are strong and deep. I grow stronger through adversity.

THE TREE OF LIFE

An internet search will yield a wealth of information regarding the tree of life. From the Kabbalistic mystic teachings to the ancient Sumerians, the tree is a well-conceived metaphor for the purpose of Life. For our purposes, as it relates to business, we will discuss the tree as it relates to ascension.

The definition of ascension is the act of rising to a higher purpose, a higher level. Given the current state of how we wheel and deal and negotiate, the need for ascension has never been greater. I believe the tree of life is a beautiful blueprint for us to follow.

The essence of the wisdom teachings of the tree is the idea that we are the bridge between the above and the below, the branches and the roots. Our physical bodies are the trunks and the bridge between these energies. You'll see this referenced in DaVinci's Vetruvian man and in numerous works of art throughout the ages. This is not a new idea. So, if we consider that our businesses are the bodies of ideas and creation—the trunks if you will—then our businesses are also the bridge to ascension. And, when most of us spend the best part of our days at work and working on our businesses, we should strive to align our purpose with our work instead of leaving it as an afterthought or merely a side project.

The image of the tree of life shows deep roots that mirror the reach and breadth of its branches and demonstrates the balance required for growth. Our cultural norm is that of imbalance. Despite that women make up nearly 50% of the workforce, they are massively underrepresented around the decision tables. Black and brown people have even less representation around these same tables which further perpetuates the imbalance. We reward growth at all costs and diminish the importance of grounding. We must center ourselves and re-member that our businesses can provide the important roots for us to increase our vibration and consciousness for the greater good.

If the trunk of the tree is the body of the business, then what parts do the balanced branches and roots represent? The saying, "As above so below," is understood that our aim is to create balance, harmony, and unity in this life. The branches reach for the stars and represent growth that comes with wisdom and experience. As mentioned in nearly every world religion there is some sort of connection to the tree from the Tree of Life in Eden mentioned in Genesis 2:8-9, the source of eternal life, to ancient Sumerian, Buddhism, Judaism, Paganism, Kabbalism, and Celtic traditions. There's no doubt the tree has significance and has withstood the test of time. It's a beautiful reminder of our individuality and the very process of manifestation from seedling to bearing fruit. The roots, often unseen, are anchored deep within the earth, and provide the stability and grounding for the branches to reach higher and higher. Since it's such a universal symbol throughout time of life itself, it's also a reminder that there is not one single path to follow to get to our destination. We must honor the numerous traditions with curiosity and reverence as others root and rise on their journey.

JOURNAL PROMPTS

1. What is my understanding of ascension?
2. Where am I reaching in my business?
3. How am I rooting in my business?
4. Is my leadership team and organization balanced?
5. What can I restore balance to my team?

MEDITATION

Come to a quiet, seated pose. Exhale down your spine and imagine a root digging deeply into the earth. Anchor this root and imagine sister roots stretching far and wide under the dirt. Inhale deeply and find extra length in your spine, reaching tall through the crown.

Begin to connect with your breath and feel the air entering and leaving your nose. Begin to relax your face and unclench your jaw as you begin to relax all of your muscles. Once you begin to soften in your body, bring your awareness to the space between your brows. Begin to imagine a tree. Visualize the shape of your tree of life. Notice the colors, size and type of your tree. Pay attention to your roots and how the tree has anchored itself in the ground. What do the branches of your tree look like? Are there any symbols that arise? How does the tree you see before you reflect your business?

Return to your breath and feel the air entering and leaving your nose. Slowly blink your eyes open. Journal whatever images came to your awareness. Give gratitude for this connection.

INTENTIONAL AFFIRMATION

My business is deeply rooted, bears fruit, and is in perfect balance. My business is a reflection of my inner balance.

THE GARDEN

The metaphor of the garden in business is not a new idea, but it is a powerful visualization that should be remembered. Every idea we have is like a seed, filled with possibilities and life. We have to decide which seeds to plant, where to plant them, how to tend to and harvest them, and what types of fruit they will bear.

We reap what we sow. We need good soil. We must prune to yield more fruit. A garden needs constant tending. We don't yield fruit overnight. Reap your harvest.

It's no surprise garden metaphors ring true for entrepreneurs because they are both gardening and building a business are a lot of work, as well as rewarding. As a child, I would find a tiny square in the landscaping that I was allowed to plant. Now, this love has turned into a huge raised-bed garden that requires constant love and attention. We start from seed, amend soil, adhere to the wisdom of companion planting, and do a ton of research. We've made lots of rookie mistakes, the worst being planting our garden before we had fencing to protect the baby plants from our goats and chickens. All our plants were almost immediately eaten as soon as we turned our backs. We've also experienced setbacks with diseased beds and insects that ruined the crop. But, each year, we learn as we go, we solve the problems at hand, and become more and more competent with our understanding of how to be successful. We learn from our mistakes, and we know we are going to make them. So we are in

a perpetual state of learning and researching and solving.
We also know that what we water grows. What we pour our time and attention into will be what takes root and flourishes. As Don Miguel Ruiz states in his book, *The Four Agreements*, "One fear or doubt planted in our mind can create an endless drama of events." So, we need to remember this lesson as we are intentional about which seeds we plant, whether they are seeds of love and possibility, or if they are seeds of fear and chaos. It's up to us to be mindful about the gardens we are creating.

JOURNAL PROMPTS

1. How does my business align with nature's cycles?
2. What is the natural rhythm of my business?
3. How can I incorporate nature into my business environment?
4. Who are the members in my guild?
5. Where are my business roots? Is this aligned with the original intention for the business?

MEDITATION

Come to a quiet, seated pose. Exhale down your spine and imagine a root digging deeply into the earth. Anchor this root and imagine sister roots stretching far and wide under the dirt. Inhale deeply and find extra length in your spine, reaching tall through the crown.

Begin to connect with your breath and feel the air entering and leaving your nose. Begin to relax your face and unclench your jaw as you begin to relax all of your muscles. Once you begin to soften in your body, bring your awareness to the space between your brows. Begin to imagine your business as a garden. What seeds have the most potential to bear fruit? What areas of your garden have weeds, need pruning, need more sun or water?

Return to your breath and feel the air entering and leaving your nose. Slowly blink your eyes open. Journal whatever images came to your awareness. Give gratitude for this insight.

INTENTIONAL AFFIRMATION

I water the seeds of the greatest good.

THE SPIDER WEB

The image of the spider web is one that I refer to time and time again as it relates to business. A web is the embodiment of the importance of carefully connecting the dots from thread to thread to create a structure that will serve its function—feeding the spider. We build businesses for lots of reasons, but first and foremost, our businesses provide financial stability. Understanding the web helps us do this.

Let's take a look at the anatomy of a spider web. Depending on the size and needs of the business, will determine how wide the anchor threads need to be. The larger the reach, the more people to provide for, the bigger the web. The spider knows how wide the net needs to be cast and starts with the threads that will provide the bridge and the framework to support the rest of the structure. I like to think of these support threads as the community our business is a part of. These threads are strong and support the entire web.

The radius threads come next. They aren't sticky, they start from the inside out and serve to connect the spiral threads. The spider walks along these threads so she doesn't get entangled on her own silk. The radius threads represent the systems our business has in place to support and efficiently enable the business to function as its intended. The radius threads help us optimize our building so we can be efficient in our effort.

Next, the auxiliary spirals. These are non-sticky spirals that serve as the reference or pattern for the capture spirals. These spirals represent the need to test, to prepare, to plan before we implement. These spirals are our experience, our network, and everything we bring to the table to allow us to lay down the sticky threads that will capture our meal.

Finally, the capture spiral is woven, round and round to create the formation that will entangle prey as they land on the web. These are the only sticky threads on the structure and function to ensure that we not only capture our meal, but also eat.

Many spiders also create floating threads of silk that shine in the sun and lure prey to their web so they increase their odds of attracting the right kind of prey. These threads are our marketing. They are intended to attract, to lure, and to capture attention. They are a critical component of the web when we become proactive about finding our meal. Otherwise, we rely on the serendipity of our prey flying directly to us. The magic of the web is in these threads.

What I love most about the spider web as a metaphor for building business is the notion that there is no wrong way of building. The spider builds a new web every day if needed. It's different in design but follows the same universal pattern. There is a formula she uses, but the actual web is unique to her building, bigger or smaller, depending on the immediate needs and her appetite.

So why are we so hyper focused that all of our businesses need to follow a 10x growth pattern in order to be funded? Is it not possible to review business viability as it relates to hunger or the problem it's solving and right sizing the effort? There isn't a one size fits all model, in fact, some of the most effective webs are small and strategically built in nooks and corners.

Often during meditation, I'll get images of webs. Sometimes we travel along the same path as other spiders and our webs are interconnected, and sometimes the webs are completely unrelated. One of my favorite quotes by Chief Seattle sums up the importance of understanding our relationships to webs. "Humankind has not woven the web of life. We are but one thread within it. Whatever we do to the web, we do to ourselves. All things are bound together. All things connect." Whether we are exclusively online or not, our businesses are connected to our communities, our customers, and the structures surrounding us. We can not isolate any of these without affecting the stability and strength of the web. Our job as leaders, entrepreneurs and visionaries is to understand this importance, to clearly connect the dots that will provide the best structure and to remember our interconnectedness. All threads lead home.

JOURNAL PROMPTS

1. What are my needs for this business?
2. Is my business framework aligned with the needs of my business?
3. What systems do I have in place to support the business?

4. What is sticky about my business?

5. How am I attracting people to my business?

MEDITATION

Come to a quiet, seated pose. Exhale down your spine and imagine a root digging deeply into the earth. Anchor this root and imagine sister roots stretching far and wide under the dirt. Inhale deeply and find extra length in your spine, reaching tall through the crown.

Begin to connect with your breath and feel the air entering and leaving your nose. Begin to relax your face and unclench your jaw as you begin to relax all of your muscles. Once you begin to soften in your body, bring your awareness to the space between your brows. Imagine the structure of your business and visualize how far it needs to extend to reach the people you need to reach. Imagine the structures that need to be in place for you to build a solid web. Imagine the threads that will make people want to stick around. Imagine what you're doing to attract people to you.

Return to your breath and feel the air entering and leaving your nose. Slowly blink your eyes open. Journal whatever images came to your awareness. Give gratitude for this insight.

INTENTIONAL AFFIRMATION

I build my web with purpose and intention.

"Your vision will become clear only when you look into your heart. Who looks outside, dreams; who looks inside, awakens."

—CARL JUNG

THE HEART OF IT ALL

This is a bittersweet topic for me. I've spent a large portion of my career trying to convince others the importance of pouring our heart and souls into their projects. Until very recently, the emotional approach was deemed soft or fluffy since results are more difficult to track in data. As a successful brand builder, I know you get the best results when the tide begins to lift all boats. The sales team starts to get returned calls, the digital marketers see an uptick in their open rates, social media stats start to improve. What we are going to talk about is just plain old difficult to measure, but that doesn't make it any less true.

Let's speak candidly, feelings have no place around today's business table. When we speak the language of feelings and emotions, we better have a graph or a data story to back up what we are saying. We will be laughed out of the room at best, at worst marginalized and replaced. But, our bodies are intelligent, we've just numbed the skill of listening to what it has to share. We often feel things before we understand or comprehend them. We all feel things differently but the metaphors of gut feeling, feeling in my bones, blood boiling, skin crawling, heart aching, and on and on are actual reminders that our bodies can guide us if we allow them to do so.

One of the benefits of being a yogi in business is that my practice on the mat of uniting the body, breath, and mind helps to reawaken this body intelligence. Yoga is obviously not the only way of doing so but it is what I have personally experienced and understand enough to share. There have been many times when I could feel whether or not something was going to work, and when asked why I thought so I tried to pull up a past experience with another project that was similar to share the outcome, the failures and why we were headed down a rocky path. I didn't have the courage to say, "Because I feel it in my bones."

The problem is that data lies. Data is only as good as the fortune teller who is able to accurately tell the number story. We are often missing critical pieces of information and end up relying on our gut or best guess anyhow. Now I know that the value of this personal body data, especially when used alongside user data and behavioral metrics, is a powerful combination. Everyone wins when we learn to cultivate body awareness and body trust so we can harness the power of our feelings.

Any marketer worth their salt understands the path to creating a loyal customer base is through the heart. We tell connective stories that will allow people to see themselves reflected in the brand. We do this through aspirational messages, inspiration, education, and love. Yes, I just said love. Loyalty comes from trust,

trust comes from familiarity, and familiarity comes from exposure. When we expose our hearts, share our love for the people we serve, they feel seen. Being seen is the very core of the human experience; it's the common thread that links us all together in this collective experience. So why do businesses shrug their shoulders and shift in their shoes at the thought of loving our people well? Because it sounds soft. It's not something that is taught in business school and there is no associated key performance indicator (KPI) for how to measure love. Yet, without heart, we're playing a short game. Loving our employees, our customers, our partners hard is the single most important thing we can do for the health of our business.

The sooner a business can find its collective heartbeat, the more likely they will succeed. It is no small feat to get a group of people pointing their arrows toward the same target. So the ability of a leader to be able to create a rhythm for the organization to synchronize to is one of the indicators I've witnessed that will determine whether or not the company will make it. Once we are able to create a singular heartbeat as an organization, we then harmonize with our customers. What do they care about? What makes them tick? It's no surprise the language we use to understand our customers all centers around the heart. Leading with the heart is much more than the next passing business trend. When an empowered team knows they can go inside, create quiet space for reflection, and have the courage (remember the Lion from Wizard of Oz taught us that courage comes from the heart), we don't succumb to external pressures who tell us to zig when we know to zag. Heart-driven leaders make great employers and create organizations where people thrive and bring their best selves to the project. We all know the high cost of employee turnover when information and intellectual property (IP) runs out the door because people don't feel valued and respected.

Businesses that lead with the heart are not weak; they are remembering the very nature of what a business is, a collection of humans coming together to solve and build together. We need both the head and heart to thrive; the collective body of the business fails when the heart does not beat.

When we care deeply about the people we work with and for, we will find mutually beneficial solutions, deeper integrations, and add that beautiful layer of thoughtfulness and intention to the tasks at hand.

JOURNAL PROMPTS

1. Can you define the collective heartbeat or mission of your company?
2. How do you connect emotionally with your customers?
3. How do your employees express feelings at work?
4. How can you create safety for expression of body intelligence?
5. How can you cultivate body intelligence in your organization?

MEDITATION

Come to a quiet, seated pose. Exhale down your spine and imagine a root digging deeply into the earth. Anchor this root and imagine sister roots stretching far and wide under the dirt. Inhale deeply and find extra length in your spine, reaching tall through the crown.

Begin to connect with your breath and feel the air entering and leaving your nose. Begin to relax your face and unclench your jaw as you begin to relax all of your muscles. Once you begin to soften in your body, bring your awareness to the space between your brows.Concentrate here until you are able to focus your energy into a single point in your third eye, or ajna chakra. Now drop this focus into your heart. Concentrate and focus all your energy in the heart. Ask yourself, "What have I been unwilling to see?"

Return to your breath and feel the air entering and leaving your nose. Slowly blink your eyes open. Journal whatever images came to your awareness. Give gratitude for this insight.

INTENTIONAL AFFIRMATION

I see and feel deeply. This care is reflected in all aspects of my business.

"Success is making those who believed in you look brilliant."

-DHARMESH SHAH

INTENTIONAL MARKETING

Intentional marketing is our way to create a thoughtful, meaningful relationship with our customers. Let's break the conversation into five main pillars: messaging, branding, content, experience, and nurture marketing. We will discuss the importance of goodness loops and how to incorporate them into your marketing strategies. There are tons of other areas of marketing such as advertising, collateral, digital, public relations, social media, and more. However, for the sake of our discussion here, we will think of those ideas as methods of distribution or amplification. Keep in mind that the essence of marketing is a series of conversations we are having with our "people" (whether we've met them or not!) at the right place and right moment in our relationship with them.

First, we must acknowledge that our digital world is incredibly distracting. We carry around the ultimate distraction box—our phone—that gives us access to the entire world in our pocket. It's difficult to get someone's attention, let alone keep it and start a meaningful conversation. This is important to understand, because as we grow brands and businesses, we need to be aware of the mindset of the people we are trying to reach from the beginning. Our messaging can only connect when we speak the language our customer understands.

In 1999, I started working at A&R Partners, a boutique high tech public relations firm in Silicon Valley. This was during the height of the dot com boom in the middle of where it was all happening. What I learned during this time and this experience was the power of "third party validation" in every single marketing effort. The very heart of any intentional marketing strategy are the people. The people who use the product. The people who have problems and the people who are solving the problems and are willing and able to give a hand back to teach and share with others how to do the same. This lens of creating and bringing humanity forward and through rich narratives will help to connect your marketing messages with your customers and create loyalty.

Reciprocity is also at the heart of any intentional marketing strategy. I personally follow the mantra of giving more to my partners than I'll ever ask in return. I communicate this to my team with the simple formula; give, give, ask. By the time we ask for help, feedback, or even the sale, we've earned the chance to do so. Reciprocity has its roots in the understanding that we are interconnected and that what's good for you is also good for me.

Most marketers understand reciprocity meaning that you give in order to receive. However, I think this is misguided and often manipulative. We do not want to obligate someone to participate in our request, we want to earn it. This is a significant difference because of the energy associated with the exchange and the lingering effects when we don't show up authentically in our relationships. And remember, we have a relationship with our customers and prospects so we want to ensure we nurture and care for our people over the long haul. Reciprocity can come in numerous forms such as training, gifting, special offers, VIP access, or any type of service that gives. An example of mutual benefit from giving more than we ask is when our customers become "product smart" and eventually evangelize the brand since they have received the white glove treatment.

When we do make our ask, I've found the practice of clear, concise communication that articulates why I'm asking has won fans and friends alike. It may sound something like, "I'm interested in having a conversation about how our product/service can help your audience. We know these people are looking for a solution for (problem) and I believe we can help each other better serve their needs." Essentially, here's what I'm looking for that makes you a valuable partner, here's what I have to share or contribute in return. If these needs are aligned, everyone wins. You know your strategy is working when people are happy to help you and are eager to return the favor.

MESSAGING

Intentional messaging is an art form. It's a process of discovery to uncover what your customers and potential customers actually care about. It's about digging into the root of why, how, who, and what. It's about taking the time to understand how your customers or prospects feel about the problems your business and products aim to solve. There is a common saying in the startup world about whether your business is a painkiller or a vitamin. Arguably, painkillers are necessary, while vitamins are supplementary. Intentional messaging translates the emotional and physical needs of the customer into words. It addresses the core wound, the pain, the heartburn, and is the very hook needed to communicate that you and your customer are aligned. You are worthy of their time and attention.

In Don Miguel Ruiz' book, *The Four Agreements*, the first agreement is to be impeccable with your word. Our words are how we express our creative power and how we are able to manifest our visions and desires. Ruiz writes, "Your word is the gift that comes directly from God. The Gospel of John in the Bible, speaking of the creation of the Universe, says, 'In the beginning was the word, and the word was with God, and the word is God.'"

When we understand the alchemy behind why this matters, we can bring a layer of deeper intent to our method. As thoughts are created in the mind, the way these thoughts become manifest is through the vibration of speech, the actual sound waves that are created when our thoughts transform into words. Science teaches us that energy never ceases, so these sound waves that we create through our words will ripple into the Universe for infinity. Therefore, when our words don't align with our core values and the language that our customer speaks and understands, we create more chaos and confusion.

Our words matter. Every single one of them. When we take this level of care and thoughtfulness about what we say and how we say it, we begin to understand the true implications of them. We know that our messaging is the very foundation of every piece of marketing that is created. We become hyper consistent with these words knowing that when we deviate from them, we make it difficult to break through the noise and land where we want them to land.

The process for coming to the right words is an ever-evolving one, but it starts with deep and active listening. When we become actively engaged in the industry in which we want to be part, we are able to identify who will be the voices that we turn to. It creates the ability to dial into the conversations that are being had around us, all to determine how and where we can plug into it and add value. When businesses don't fully immerse themselves in the heart and the mind of the people they serve, everything falls flat. It's really important to speak the language of your customer, and we often understand this nomenclature through an uncovering of user personas and archetypes.

THE ARCHETYPES

Many marketers employ the use of archetypes and personas. The most commonly practiced archetypes relate to the twelve Jungian archetypes, defined by Carl Jung in his book, *Archetypes and the Collective Unconscious*. At the highest level, archetypes can be understood as universal energies that inform, inspire, and potentially interfere in our lives. It's my understanding that archetypes are like great winds that influence our behavior and drive our unconscious behaviors. For instance, Caroline Myss, in her book called *Sacred Contracts*, identifies four primary archetypes: the child, the victim, the prostitute, and the saboteur.

Every human has aspects of these Universal energies that we may present at different times in our lives. Where this becomes insightful as we develop connective marketing messaging, is when we can translate this knowledge into words and emotions that express the deepest aspects of ourselves. When aware of archetypes and how they inform the lives of our customers, it gives us a more complex and rich layer of information so our messaging speaks to their greatest fears and/or their most aspirational selves.

I strongly encourage a deeper dive into this topic since this psychology is well-studied and should be understood and investigated in depth. However, the common archetypes are grouped to symbolize basic human motivation. The very core of all marketing efforts is to drive the behavior we desire based on our business goals. So it's critical to understand who you are talking with and what motivates them. The twelve archetypes as defined by Jung are:

1. **The Innocent:** Exhibits happiness, goodness, optimism, safety, romance, and youth. Example brand: Dove

2. **The Everyman:** Seeks connections and belonging; is recognized as supportive, faithful and down-to-earth. Example brands include: Home Depot

3. **The Hero:** On a mission to make the world a better palace, the Hero is courageous, bold, inspiration. Example brand: Nike.

4. **The Rebel:** Questions authority and breaks the rules; the Rebel craves freedom and revolution. Example brand: Harley-Davison

5. **The Explorer:** Finds inspiration in travel, risk, discovery, and the thrill of new experiences. Example brand: Jeep

6. **The Creator:** Imaginative, inventive and driven to build things of enduring meaning and value. Example brand: Lego

7. **The Ruler:** Creates order from the chaos, the Ruler is typically controlling and stern, yet responsible and organized. Example brand: Verizon

8. **The Magician:** Wishes to create something special and make dreams a reality, the Magician is seen as visionary and spiritual. Example brand: Disney

9. **The Lover:** Creates intimate moments, inspires love, passion, romance and commitment. Example brand includes: Victoria's Secret

10. **The Caregiver:** Protects and cares for others, is compassionate, nurturing and generous. Example brand: Johnson & Johnson

11. **The Jester:** Brings joy to the world through humor, fun, irreverence and often likes to make some mischief. M&M's

12. **The Sage:** Committed to helping the world gain deeper insight and wisdom, the Sage serves as the thoughtful mentor or advisor. Example brand: Google

The word persona actually is a derivative of the latin word meaning a "theatrical mask." Therefore, in intentional marketing, we connect to the actual "person" we are trying to reach and create messaging that is reflective of our customer's highest self, not just the masks they wear. Let's be clear, we all wear masks, but we aim to go deeper into understanding true motivation.

Whenever I begin the process of creating intentional messaging for my clients, I seek to truly understand the people they serve. I speak to actual customers and prospects and pay close attention to the words they choose and how they use them. I try to weave this language into the messaging so our customer can "hear their own voice" from our brand.

We must strive to leverage the wisdom of Jung's archetypes, yet layer the human element on top of these insights, so we don't forget that our business exists because of the customers the business serves. In our data-driven world, it is easy to replace a human face with ones and zeros. It is easy to count an action as a click or a like, instead of what it truly is, a person on the other end of our communication either doing or not doing what we wish them to do. Therefore, we can create mindful messages when we connect our words and value with the people we are building for.

To create intentional messaging we should read and have knowledge of some of the psychologists who have studied the mind and the secrets behind motivation: Jung, Maslow, Hertzberg, McClellan, Vroom, and McGregor. As discussed, Jung explores archetypes and our primitive psyche as a basis for influencing behavior. Maslow breaks down our hierarchy of needs. Hertzberg introduced the two-factor theory of extrinsic versus intrinsic motivational factors. McClelland's Human Motivation Theory and Vroom's Expectancy Theory and McGregor's Theory X and Theory Y dive into how to lead teams and motivate certain behaviors.

Although these theories are primarily focused on motivating teams and employees, it's good to have a solid grasp of psychology and how to motivate and influence others as well as investigate and try to stay current on the latest advancements in neuroscience. After all, the core of business is to motivate others to action, whether it's to subscribe, to purchase, to participate or any number of ways a business asks us to engage. The saying "knowledge is power" is a wonderful example of using this information about how to persuade and motivate for positive change instead of just playing to humanity's lower vibrational patterns of scarcity, fear, guilt, and shame. As Maya Angelou so eloquently put it, "Do the best you can until you know better. When you know better, do better."

We have a responsibility to do better and often marketers pull from the bottom of the barrel. We don't have to look too far to see this in action during any election cycle since many political ads and marketing embody these fear-based techniques.

It's common practice today to talk to our lowest selves, our ego, with tactics that tap into collective deep seated fears. Yet, we have an opportunity in business to turn this practice on its head and strive to do right by and for each other. Therefore, it's also good to have a general understanding of "Maslow's Hierarchy of Needs," which was proposed by the psychologist Abraham Maslow in 1943 in his book, A *Theory of Human Motivation*. This theory represents the five general stages people progress through in the pursuit of what they want: physiology, safety, belongingness/love, esteem, and self-actualization. The more we know and understand the person we are speaking to, and the stage of their life journey, the more we understand what makes them tick and what will motivate them to act. Hopefully, intentional businesses aim to provide products and services aligned with real problems that are truly valuable. When we raise the bar and our expectations for each other, we can begin to have a conversation that is connective and reciprocal yet still effective and productive.

As we know, everything in life and business is in constant motion and in constant transformation. As we learn and get closer to the hearts and needs of our people, our messaging can and should evolve with this wisdom. In doing so, we must never forget the importance of being impeccable with our words, to choose them carefully, knowing that the vibrations we create will have long standing implications not only for ourselves, our customers and also the world.

JOURNAL PROMPTS

1. Who is your customer and what do they care most about?
2. How does your business solve their needs?
3. Are your words true? Are your words clear? Do you express yourself in truth?
4. Does your messaging connect with your customer?
5. Are your words aligned with your business intent?

MEDITATION

Come to a quiet, seated pose. Exhale down your spine and imagine a root digging deeply into the earth. Anchor this root and imagine sister roots stretching far and wide under the dirt. Inhale deeply and find extra length in your spine, reaching tall through the crown.

Begin to imagine an actual person or customer your business solves for. Identify who the person is and pay close attention to the details of the person. What do they look like? How do they dress? How do they carry themselves? Where do they live? What are they struggling with? Where do they succeed? What causes them pain? What brings them joy? Where does your business fit into their life? How can you help this person?

Return to your breath and feel the air entering and leaving your nose. Slowly blink your eyes open. Journal whatever images came to your awareness.

INTENTIONAL AFFIRMATION

My words are clear and magnetic and attract the right people to my business.

BRANDING

Prior to my career in public relations, I worked as an art dealer. Therefore, the visual representation of branding is my swansong. Creating a logo, along with a business card, is often the first step for entrepreneurs since it makes the business feel official and legit. This is more than mere perception; branding is the external representation of the heart of the business. So, creating that logo actually does breathe life into the idea, gives the business an official beat, and puts a stake in the ground about who you are and why you exist.

The history of branding, according to Douglas Rushkoff in his book, *Life Inc. How the World Became A Corporation and How to Take it Back*, breaks branding down as the way we replaced the human face of the business when we moved to a model where the individual was no longer able to serve the customers directly. He gives a great example of the Quaker on the box of our oatmeal. His role in branding is to instill the same trust you had with the product as when you would have a personal interaction, face to face. Branding is about recreating this feeling and connection with our customers.

Side note: Rushkoff is a visionary and genius so I highly encourage you to read any and all of his books to better understand why it matters more than ever to bring humanity back to our businesses.

We can create feelings and connections with our customers through shapes, color, and imagery. I've always been particularly interested in the science of sacred geometry, essentially, the sacred meaning of shapes, the proportion of shapes, and the ancient symbolism and meaning of various shapes and images. Woven throughout history in architecture and art, applying the symbols and correspondences are another layer of intention you can bring to your brand. Geometry and mathematical ratios, harmonics and proportion, are also found in music and can be described as a way to speak a common language on a deeply intuitive, subconscious level. The more we understand the power of the symbolism behind certain shapes, as in sacred geometry, we can create a more thoughtful visual identity that supports the intention of the business.

The psychology of color is a well-studied field. According to *The Physics Hypertexbook* (https://physics.info/color/), "Color is a function of the human visual system, and is not an intrinsic property. Objects don't have a color, they give off light that appears to be a color. Spectral power distributions exist in the physical world, but color exists only in the mind of the beholder."

Said another way, color is the range of light that our eyes can perceive. Color theory can be a complicated and deep science, particularly as it relates to theory of the shades black, white, brown, and gray. Your answers will vary whether you are talking to an artist, a printer, a philosopher, a scientist, or a child opening a new box of crayons. This is not a comprehensive playbook about color, hues, tones, and shades but simply a reminder that when we have a deeper understanding of the nature of things, it gives us more context about the subtle ways these decisions may affect the association with and for the brand. There are competing theories and associations, so it's smart to acknowledge this, discuss implications, test, and listen to your instincts about the effectiveness of the symbols you are choosing to represent the brand.

Here is a quick guide to our emotional connection to color and the sacred vibration that color emits. Remember, as it is with words, color is also a wave. We can emit high vibration frequencies or lower frequencies based on what we are trying to accomplish. This is the essence of branding that resonates. We are aligning our vibration with the vibration of the people we are trying to attract.

COLOR	ASSOCIATION	FREQUENCY
Red	Exciting	Lowest
Orange	Friendly	
Yellow	Optimistic	
Green	Peaceful	Middle
Indigo	Creative	
Violet	Calm	Highest
TONES	**ASSOCIATION**	**FREQUENCY**
White	Simple	Mixture/reflection
Black	Sophisticated or	No frequency.
Brown	Grounded	Mixture of primary

JOURNAL PROMPTS

1. What does your current visual identity say about your business?
2. Is this aligned with your intent?
3. What changes can you make to be more clear?

MEDITATION

Come to a quiet, seated pose. Exhale down your spine and imagine a root digging deeply into the earth. Anchor this root and imagine sister roots stretching far and wide under the dirt. Inhale deeply and find extra length in your spine, reaching tall through the crown. Bring your awareness to the very tip of your nose and feel the air entering and leaving the nostrils. Feel the shift in the body as you create this breath awareness. Now bring your awareness to the space between your brows, your mental screen, and notice the first color that comes into your awareness. Is this color aligned with the associations you feel about your business? Ask yourself how your brand reflects your highest purpose.

Return to your breath and feel the air entering and leaving your nose. Slowly blink your eyes open. Journal whatever images came to your awareness.

INTENTIONAL AFFIRMATION

My brand is a beautiful reflection of my business intent. Our value is clearly articulated.

APPLYING THE SEVEN LAWS OF THE UNIVERSE AND THE CHAKRAS

Understanding color and its vibration is a perfect segue into a brief overview of the chakra system, as well as a very brief introduction to the Seven Laws of the Universe. The Laws of the Universe are also known as the Hermetic Principles, and are significant to business.

The chakras are known as energy wheels within our physical bodies. They physically range from the crown of the head to the base of the spine, or as yogis say, our root. They correspond to our organs and glands and the Seven Laws of the Universe.

The point of this information is not an in-depth study on the topic since it's intensive, deep, and takes a lifetime of study to master. Rather, it's to spark an idea and general understanding that there is so much extra thought and care we can apply to our businesses when we start to uncover symbolism and science. Applying yet another layer of intelligence can help inform the type of brand you want to create that truly represents the intent and vision of the business. Although traditional color theory and the colors associated with the seven chakras don't cleanly align, allow the information presented to guide your gut on what is the best direction to take. There are numerous ways to choose which colors should be employed to help create a connective brand. Our artistry comes into play when we move from simply shrugging shoulders or copying others to creating a palette based with intention.

Starting at the crown chakra, the associated law of the universe is mentalism. This is the understanding that the mind of the All creates everything and that the world is a reflection of this mind. The crown chakra represents the I AM, the understanding and experience of complete unity, and return to one's knowledge of Self. The associated color is white, gold, or a rainbow of all colors.

Next, our third eye is associated with the law of correspondence. It teaches us "as above so below; so below as above" as identified in The Hermeticism Collection By The Three Initiates, Hermes, Trismegistus, Manly P. Hall; there is no separation between body, soul, and spirit. Cultivating inner sight through the mind's eye creates harmony and balance in the physical, spiritual, and mental realms. The associated color is violet.

Our throat chakra corresponds to the law of vibration. We create the vibration of sound through this chakra and it is associated with truth, finding our voice, and the power of song. It tells us, "Nothing rests, everything moves, everything vibrates." When we understand the implications of the law of vibration, we harness the power of our thoughts, as understood in the book titled *The Secret*, our words and our emotions. We are able to perceive the various vibrations of the Universe through our five senses. The associated color is indigo.

Our heart chakra corresponds to the law of rhythm. "Everything flows, out and in; everything has its tides; all things rise and fall; the pendulum-swing manifests in everything; the measure of the swing to the right is the measure of the swing to the left; rhythm compensates." The heart chakra is associated with compassion, empathy, and unconditional love. Love is the path to increase our collective vibration and create Universal alignment. The associated color is green.

Our solar plexus corresponds to the law of cause and effect. "Every cause has its effect; every effect has its cause." Our vibrations condition everything in our lives. Nothing escapes this law; we are all accountable. This is the law of responsibility to ourselves and to others. The solar plexus is also our storehouse of energy, action, and will. The associated color is yellow.

Our sacral chakra corresponds to the law of polarity. The Kybalion states that, "Everything is Dual; everything has poles; everything has its pair of opposites; like and unlike are the same; opposites are identical in nature, but different in degree; extremes meet; all truths are but half-truths; all paradoxes may be reconciled." This law is the essence of creation or creativity. We must understand that everything we create has both positive and negative aspects. The sacral plexus also corresponds to our sensual energies. The associated color is orange.

Our root chakra corresponds to the law of gender. The Kybalion states that, "Gender is in everything; everything has its Masculine and Feminine Principles. Gender manifests on all planes." The root chakra corresponds with stability and safety. The associated color is red.

This is just the highest level overview of how and why branding and the colors and shapes we use to represent our brands matter greatly to create the necessary trust needed to build a successful business. In a noisier-than-ever world, design helps us keep and maintain attention—yet is often undervalued for its relative impact.

COLOR	ASSOCIATION	FREQUENCY	CHAKRA	CHAKRA COLOR MEANING	LAW
Red	Exciting	Lowest	Root	Stable	Gender
Orange	Friendly		Sacral	Creative	Polarity
Yellow	Optimistic		Solar Plexus	Powerful	Cause & Effect
Green	Peaceful	Middle	Heart	Compassionate	Rhythm
Indigo	Creative		Throat	Clear	Vibration
Violet	Calm	Highest	Third eye	Intuitive	Correspondence
TONES	ASSOCIATION	FREQUENCY	CHAKRA	CHAKRA COLOR MEANING	LAW
White	Simple		Crown	Enlightened	Mentalism
Black	Sophisticated			Shadowy	
Brown	Grounded			Earthy	

When we focus our intention through creative visualization, we leverage the laws of the universe. With a deeper understanding of the connection between color, its related chakra and the related correspondences, we can begin to access our deep and profound ability to create and manifest brands with purpose. When we access this knowledge and apply it to our businesses, we no longer become reactionary bystanders but powerful drivers of our own destinies. Branding is the process of discovering who we are and how we wish to present ourselves in the world.

JOURNAL PROMPTS

1. Do our colors align with the intent of the business?
2. What does our visual identity communicate to the world?
3. What emotions does your branding evoke?
4. Where is your branding out of sync with the laws of the universe?
5. How can you apply this information to your branding?

MEDITATION

Come to a quiet, seated pose. Exhale down your spine and imagine a root digging deeply into the earth. Anchor this root and imagine sister roots stretching far and wide under the dirt. Inhale deeply and find extra length in your spine, reaching tall through the crown.

Starting at the base of your spine, at the root chakra, imagine a red glowing ball. Silently say in your mind, I am safe. Bring your awareness to the space between your navel and your root, the sacral chakra. Imagine an orange glowing ball. Silently say to yourself, I am creative. Bring your awareness to the space just above the navel. This is the solar plexus, our storehouse of energy and will. Imagine a yellow glowing ball and silently say in your mind, I am capable. Bring your awareness to the center of your chest, your heart chakra. Imagine a green glowing ball and silently say in your mind, I am love. Bring your awareness to your throat, imagine a blue glowing ball. Silently say in your mind, I am truth. Bring your awareness to the space between your brows, your third eye chakra. Imagine a violet glowing ball and silently say in your mind, I am wisdom. Bring your awareness to the space over your head, neck and shoulders, your crown chakra. Imagine a beautiful white light, a golden halo or a rainbow of colors. Silently say in your mind, I AM.

Return to your breath and feel the air entering and leaving your nose. Slowly blink your eyes open. Journal whatever images came to your awareness.

INTENTIONAL AFFIRMATION

Energy flows clearly through every aspect of my business.

CONTENT MARKETING AND STORYTELLING

Content strategies should be aligned with the brand values and categorized into brand or content pillars. These pillars represent a body or bucket of information you are committed to talk about, create education and stories around, as well as to find experts, influencers, and co-storytellers who also care about the same or similar pillar. Content marketing sings when we bring forth our humanity and employ the power of reciprocity and shared value.

An example of successful content marketing in action is RateMyAgent's *Undisruptables* campaign. This was in response to the real estate industry trend of outside disruption that continues to threaten an individual agent's role and relevance. Instead of focusing on all the ways an agent could lose their job, the campaign focused on the things agents do to serve customers well and deliver value. It provided a mirror to other agents to see their own worth and value in their jobs as too often agents took their own gifts for granted. Video stories were told by industry influencers who were known for excellence as well as valuing customer service and relationships. This campaign immediately put this little-known brand on the map, aligned with the heart of the customer, and provided a backdrop to have a conversation about the importance of customer service to drive awareness to the launch of an industry-wide service awards program. The campaign was such a huge success, with the company achieving massive growth in just under a year.

Shining a spotlight on agents and inspiring them to be undisruptable was woven into the DNA of the overarching messaging that extends beyond the initial content parameters.

Understanding, organizing, and committing to content pillars will help create alignment with the things you care about and the things your customers care about. Content is how we magnetize or draw our people to us. It's also known as inbound marketing, but I like to call it magnetic marketing. Lots of people create content, but the difference between magnetic content and noise is in its essence. We raise the collective vibration when we shine a light on others who are doing great work, when we teach and share how to achieve success with our products or services, and when we generate goodness. Magnetic marketing has a mix of inspiration, aspiration, teaching, sharing, and shining.

SEO (search engine optimization) plays a huge role in content marketing since Google is one of the primary paths to connect your content to the eyes you are seeking to find. We have to consider not only what we create, but make it easy to access for bots and spiders to crawl and categorize. We do this through well thought out headlines aligned with how people search, URLs or slugs that are descriptive and clear, words that are aligned and associated with the topic, and valuable, authoritative content. Our words should reference and link to others who have similar value to share so we can create our own web of information that is useful to our readers.

Storytelling runs deep in our DNA. For as long as humans have been in bodies, we have likely used stories to share who we are, how we are different and the same, what we believe and do not believe, and all the great things about being alive. Connective and engaging stories do follow a pattern of weaving in five key elements: the setting, the pain, the quest, the crisis, and the new normal or solution. Great stories also have interesting characters, structure, and unexpected twists, turns, and outcomes. Done well, stories allow our people to see themselves in our content, get them interested and engaged, and eventually aligned with our mission. This is one of the reasons why RateMyAgent was such a huge success as it inspired other real estate agents to say, "Hey, that's me too" and to know they belonged.

Well-conceived content strategies (1) combine the power of influencer marketing by lifting up trusted faces and tastemakers, (2) incorporate social proof by using third parties to validate and share their experiences, and (3) written in the customer's language, connect emotionally. This is a high bar to achieve but will set your business apart as a valuable partner and worthy of their time.

JOURNAL PROMPTS

1. Define your content pillars.
2. Do your content pillars align with your brand values and your messaging?
3. How does your content add value to your customer's life?

4. Does your content employ the best practices of storytelling?

5. Is your content optimized to be found on the web?

BONUS QUESTION

How are you determining if your content is magnetizing the right people to your business?

MEDITATION

Come to a quiet, seated pose. Exhale down your spine and imagine a root digging deeply into the earth. Anchor this root and imagine sister roots stretching far and wide under the dirt. Inhale deeply and find extra length in your spine, reaching tall through the crown.

Imagine sitting around a campfire. Who is sitting with you? Notice if there is a particular person sharing a story or if everyone is contributing to the conversation. What is being shared? How does this make you feel? Ask how your business connects to this narrative.

Return to your breath and feel the air entering and leaving your nose. Slowly blink your eyes open. Journal whatever images came to your awareness.

INTENTIONAL AFFIRMATION

We clearly communicate our value.

EXPERIENTIAL AND NURTURE MARKETING

One of our primary goals as marketers is to create rich, connective experiences for our customers. We do this because when we can reach into the hearts and minds of our people, we create loyalty. Customer churn, or customer turnover, is a huge problem for most businesses and, from a sheer dollars and cents perspective, we know that it is much more costly to constantly acquire new customers than to retain and nurture the folks who have already opted in.

Experiential marketing is all about how we interact with our customers. This can be done face to face at events and trade shows, door-to-door with gifts, and when we uplevel the way we communicate with our customers via phone, email, and even social media.

The key to success with experiential marketing is to surprise and delight. Applying the understanding of surprise and delight doesn't have to be expensive, but it does need to be unexpected. The concept of surprise and delights is about exceeding expectations and going beyond the mundane to becoming remarkable. The focus is not about the actual message, but in the intent of what feeling or emotion is left behind. As Seth Godin accurately explains in a 2013 blog post titled, Different or Remarkable, "Remarkable has nothing to do with the marketer. Remarkable is in the eye of the consumer, the person who 'remarks.' If people talk about what you're doing, it's remarkable, by definition. The goal, then, isn't to draw some positioning charts and announce that you have differentiated your product. No, the opportunity is to actually create something that people choose to talk about, regardless of what the competition is doing."

Even though this was written nearly seven years ago, it's as true today as ever. Yet, many marketers forget this basic fact that we must create interesting, connective, emotive campaigns or we will never break through the noise and the clutter. Why would we even bother creating marketing material that is not going to create a magical moment for our people? Businesses often get lost in the need to communicate what; they lose the essence and the very purpose of why the product exists to begin with.

There are some basic rules of doing experiential marketing well. The first is that there cannot be any strings attached. The entire effort is to see and love our people. We are trying to create brand affinity and loyalty and nothing cheapens that faster than a hidden agenda. So, the second rule is to have crystal clear intent on why you are creating this experience. And finally, the third rule is to have fun. This is your moment to get creative, to be playful, and to celebrate the people who support your business.

Which brings us to nurture marketing. Nurture marketing is the idea that we should find a natural, authentic flow to stay connected with our customers and those that support our business. When we over or under communicate, we lose the balance needed to create loyalty and longevity. Nurture marketing is all about identifying the customer milestones and creating memorable moments throughout their journey with you. It's about celebrating accomplishments of tasks, goals reached, and acknowledging the customer as a critical component of the business.

Many small businesses have a difficult time nurturing customers because the role of the microbusiness or solopreneur is to juggle many different tasks. We wind up tackling what needs to get done today and forget about the importance of honoring those who have helped us get here. This is particularly true for many of the real estate agents and real estate brokerages I've had the pleasure of working with over the years. Even though there is a deep understanding that future business is built on the back of the relationships they maintain, very few are able to create a system to prioritize the effort. If any nurturing happens, it's often ad hoc and infrequent.

In the earliest incarnation of my product line, Intentionaliteas, we aimed to solve this problem by creating a quarterly stay-in-touch gifting platform. Agents could subscribe to a set-it-and-forget-it system to have a handwritten note, herbal tea blend, and corresponding candle delivered right to their customer's door. What I witnessed from the agents and brokerages in my pilot group was analysis paralysis. Because they were unable to determine if the gift would be well-received, they did nothing. The truth is, it doesn't really matter what the gift is, but the intent behind the gifting. This intent is where the effort often goes off the rails. The intent should be to nurture, to stay connected, and to show that you actually care about the person. This can be done with a quick text when the person pops into your mind, a short handwritten note to let them know you were thinking of them, or a popby, a small gesture of gratitude. Do not confuse gifting and nurturing with swag and promotional items. The intent is really different. There is a time and place for both, yet the emotional intelligence to discern when a gift is for us as a promotional item or for our clients is of paramount importance. Swag clearly falls into the marketing and advertising bucket, and should not be counted as nurture marketing. You could convince me otherwise if you also include a personalized, handwritten note along with the item.

And as for the Intentionaliteas stay-in-touch system? We pivoted from this direction and now offer a one-time gift option based on the intention you want to send: Love, Peace, Gratitude, Home, and Wellness. This seems to be the perfect blend of an affordable, personal yet professional touch that meets our customer's needs.

Let's be clear, our businesses exist for the sole purpose of serving our customers' needs. This idea can be lost along the way, so nurture marketing puts this idea front and center. Nurture marketing starts on day one and exists for the lifetime of the relationship. These are not campaigns per say, although isolated campaigns can be woven into nurture marketing, but it is an ongoing conversation you have with a person you deeply care about.

Examples of nurture marketing include: onboarding and product training; celebration of personal events such as birthdays, anniversaries, first meetings; and celebrations of key moments.

Nurture marketing can be gifts, cards, thoughtful notes, phone calls, texts, or any kind of outreach as long as the intent is to show you care. Nurture marketing is not about asking for business or selling anything, it's about showing up as a valued partner. Nurture marketing is about spreading love that will raise the collective vibration. It's about seeing your people well and is an investment in the longevity of your business.

JOURNAL PROMPTS

1. What are the experiences you are creating for your customers?
2. When was the last time you employed the principles of surprise and delight?
3. How do your reviews reflect your core values? What do your customers say about your business?
4. What is your customer retention rate?
5. How can you implement experiential and nurture marketing into your overall business strategy?

MEDITATION

Come to a quiet, seated pose. Exhale down your spine and imagine a root digging deeply into the earth. Anchor this root and imagine sister roots stretching far and wide under the dirt. Inhale deeply and find extra length in your spine, reaching tall through the crown.

Begin to connect with your breath and feel the air entering and leaving your nose. Begin to relax your face and unclench your jaw as you begin to relax all of your muscles. Once you begin to soften in your body, bring your awareness to the space between your brows. Who is the first person to show up on your mental screen? Is it someone you know? Is it someone who is unknown to you? Who or what do they represent? Do they have a special message for you?

Return to your breath and feel the air entering and leaving your nose. Slowly blink your eyes open. Journal whatever images came to your awareness. Send a handwritten note, text, or Intentionaliteas gift box to the person who showed up for you to let them know you were thinking of them.

INTENTIONAL AFFIRMATION

My business creates surprise and delight with every experience.

GOODNESS LOOPS

I like to think of goodness loops as the ways our business can give back. Generosity and joy help to raise our vibration, so it's important to incorporate goodness into our business strategies. One of the easiest ways to create a goodness loop is to allocate a portion of profit to a charity or cause that is aligned with the mission of the company. This works because it incorporates the ideals of shared value, reciprocity, and gains you access to and camaraderie with audiences who have common interests.

It's becoming increasingly more common for businesses to donate a portion of profits to aligned causes and charities. A few of my favorite examples of brands with charitable goodness loops are Warby Parker, a glasses company that donates a pair of glasses to someone in need with every purchase, as well as Tom's who does the same for a pair of shoes. The buy one, give one model is a powerful way to encourage consumers to promote their social consciousness with their purchase power. We are finally able to create a goodness loop through Intentionaliteas as we began to create custom tea blends aligned with specific causes. Love Tea supports Glennon Doyles' non-profit organization called Together Rising because she calls her pride, Love Warriors. Equalitea supports leveling the playing field for young black lives, Humanitea gives back to LGBTQ causes, and so on and so forth. We chose to donate 10% of online profits to these causes that our business cares about because we could commit to this amount. It doesn't really matter how much you donate, but be consistent and transparent. There are potential tax implications for charitable giving, so check with your accountant to ensure you understand the associated laws.

Ponysaurus, a craft brewing company based in Durham, North Carolina, does an excellent job of creating goodness loops in the business model. A self-described community company that happens to sell beer, they creates special blends that support the community. Don't Be Mean to People: A Golden Rule Saison brew arose in response to HB2, or North Carolina's "bathroom bill." Taking a stand on this issue that was aligned with their brand values, attracted like-minded customers and created brand loyalty, as well as a ton of publicity. Doing good is good for business!

Another goodness loop to consider is regarding the waste or the extra our businesses produce. In every business we must consider the waste that we create and our obligation to responsibly address it. We must be intentional not only about what we produce but also about what we throw away. Our waste creates an opportunity to determine if there is possibility for use elsewhere. Are there scraps that can be repurposed into something useful for someone else? How can we counteract the effects of our businesses on the planet? Do we plant trees? Do we participate or create a water cleanup effort? When we take a hard look at the output of our businesses and honestly acknowledge our waste, we are able to counter the ill effect with a positive solution.

Goodness loops can also be created to support the health and well-being of our co-builders or employees. We can create opportunities for continuing education, create policies that support the value of retreats and sabbaticals, or have generous work-rest-play benefits. We can create spaces within our buildings that support the entire person such as greenrooms, meditation spaces, and libraries.

Thinking beyond our employees as numbers and output, can help us create goodness loops that enrich and empower the people who we've chosen to link arms with. There are some businesses that help systemize this process for your company such as GoodCompany.org, Gvinga, and one of my personal favorites, Giveback Homes.

JOURNAL PROMPTS

1. Do you have a giveback strategy?
2. How can generosity and joy improve your business?
3. Identify the waste your business generates?
4. How can this waste be transformed?
5. Does your business environment support the whole person?

MEDITATION

Come to a quiet, seated pose. Exhale down your spine and imagine a root digging deeply into the earth. Anchor this root and imagine sister roots stretching far and wide under the dirt. Inhale deeply and find extra length in your spine, reaching tall through the crown.

Begin to connect with your breath and feel the air entering and leaving your nose. Begin to relax your face and unclench your jaw as you begin to relax all of your muscles. Once you begin to soften in your body, bring your awareness to the space between your eyebrows. Allow your mind to drift to a cause you care deeply about. Begin to visualize how your business could support this cause. What does it look like? Who is participating? What is the outcome?

Return to your breath and feel the air entering and leaving your nose. Slowly blink your eyes open. Journal whatever images came to your awareness.

INTENTIONAL AFFIRMATION

My business is generous and good.

"In every ending is a new beginning."

—UNKNOWN

PULLING IT TOGETHER

As many of us are craving a new path to purpose and prosperity, we can look to yoga and spiritual wisdom as a guide. This is independent of any religion or dogma, as it focuses on Universal knowledge of self awareness, self realization, and our ability to create and manifest with intention.

The heart of the intentional business is about reconnecting to the natural rhythms, to resonate with our customers, and to find our collective heartbeat, all of which can be done when we slow down, pay attention, and re-member.

With the knowledge that our businesses are a reflection of our inner selves, we can finally embrace the power and the importance of changing our current culture and building new tables together that are aligned with the greatest good. We should always be asking questions, we just need to know the right questions to ask. The answers exist within us and will awaken us to our true power. This curiosity will guide us to a path of purpose and prosperity.

Who am I?

What is my purpose?

What was I born to do?

What are my gifts?

What was the life I was born to live?

What is the purpose of my business?

How can my business serve the greatest good?

How can I be more intentional with my business?

MEDITATION

Find a comfortable seat, close your eyes and begin to connect to the rhythms of your breath. Bring your awareness to your heart center. Imagine a bright, glowing light. With each inhale, the light grows brighter. With each exhale, we release and return the light to the world. Sit and bring your focus to this beautiful, balanced exchange of energy. Pay attention to any shifts in your awareness as you let your light grow and expand until it envelopes your entire body. Slowly return to your normal breath and offer gratitude for this moment, this breath, and the light that is growing inside you. Journal any visions that may have come to you.

INTENTIONAL AFFIRMATION

My business reflects the highest good. My business has purpose and is abundantly prosperous.

FINAL THOUGHTS

We often spend our best and most productive hours working. For many of us, this time is given to our work, not to our families and loved ones for a significant portion of our lives. Yet, our culture has taught us to decouple our highest, spiritual selves from this effort, leaving a gap and deep longing within. My hope in writing this book is to share some of the lessons I've learned along the way to spark your curiosity and to uncover how to be more intentional with the precious hours of this lifetime we've been gifted. It is a journey of discovery with lots of twists and turns along the way. Of all the life lessons, asking questions and learning to listen to your own inner teacher, may be the most important. Trust that you have everything you need—just as the giant oak sleeps within the acorn.

Made in United States
Orlando, FL
29 September 2023